Happiness

Happiness

How to Get into the Habit of Being Happy

Gill Hasson

CAPSTONE
A Wiley Brand

This edition first published 2018.

© 2018 Gill Hasson

Registered office

John Wiley & Sons Ltd, The Atrium, Southern Gate, Chichester, West Sussex, PO19 8SQ, United Kingdom

For details of our global editorial offices, for customer services and for information about how to apply for permission to reuse the copyright material in this book please see our website at www.wiley.com.

Wiley publishes in a variety of print and electronic formats and by print-on-demand. Some material included with standard print versions of this book may not be included in e-books or in print-on-demand. If this book refers to media such as a CD or DVD that is not included in the version you purchased, you may download this material at http://booksupport.wiley.com. For more information about Wiley products, visit www.wiley.com.

Library of Congress Cataloging-in-Publication Data

Names: Hasson, Gill, author.
Title: Happiness : how to get into the habit of being happy / Gill Hasson.
Description: Chichester, West Sussex, United Kingdom : John Wiley & Sons Ltd., 2018. | Includes index. |
Identifiers: LCCN 2018026832 (print) | ISBN 9780857087591 (pbk.)
Subjects: LCSH: Happiness.
Classification: LCC BF575.H27 H384 2018 (print) | DDC 158—dc23
LC record available at https://lccn.loc.gov/2018026832

A catalogue record for this book is available from the British Library.

ISBN 978-0-857-08759-1 (pbk)
ISBN 978-0-857-08762-1 (ebk)
ISBN 978-0-857-08756-0 (ebk)

Cover design: Wiley

Set in 12/15 pt SabonLTStd-Roman by Aptara Inc., New Delhi, India

Printed in Great Britain by TJ International Ltd, Padstow, Cornwall, UK

To Tom with love from Mum xx

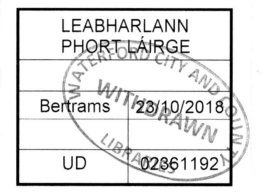

Contents

Introduction   1

1   What Happiness Is   9
2   How to Be Happy: Find Purpose and
     Meaning   23
3   Step Out of Your Comfort Zone   61
4   How to Be Happy: Identify and Indulge
     in Small Pleasures   85
5   Happiness When Life Is Really Hard   117
6   How to Help Others Be Happy   139

Useful Websites and Books   159
About the Author   163
Index   165

Introduction

Folks are usually about as happy as they make their minds up to be.

— Abraham Lincoln

We may all have different abilities, interests and lifestyles, goals, values, beliefs, and expectations, but there's one thing that we all have in common: we want to be happy.

How happy are you right now? How happy are you with your life in general, as a whole? Would you like to be happier? How much happier? Of course, it's not really possible to measure happiness; there's no point system or way to measure the happiness flowing through your bloodstream. But we don't really need to be able to measure happiness in order to know whether we're happy or not. And it seems that so many of us aren't.

Levels of anxiety, stress, loneliness, and depression appear to have escalated in recent years. The mental health charity Mind reports that, in England, one in six people report experiencing a common mental health problem (such as anxiety or depression) in any given week. A survey of 2330 people in the UK carried out in 2014 by YouGov for The Mental Health Foundation revealed that almost one in five people feel anxious 'nearly all of the time' or 'a lot of the time'.

A survey carried out in the UK in 2017 for the Jo Cox Commission on Loneliness showed that almost three-quarters of older people in the UK are lonely – but anyone who is socially isolated as a result of, for example, the loss of family and friends, unemployment, a disability, illness, or caring for others can also experience the unhappiness that comes with feelings of loneliness.

Even if you aren't lonely or experiencing a mental health problem – even if your life is OK – it seems that the pressure to be happy and successful is greater than ever before. These days, it's not just having money, a great job, a nice home, a good relationship, and lots of friends that defines a successful life, but how happy you are and how often you're happy.

For many of us, it's become important to appear super happy all the time; to share happy news, post happy photos, tweet happy tweets. Due to social media's obsession with joy, it can seem like everyone else is achieving nirvana levels of happiness and bliss. In fact, a 2017 poll by the charity Girlguiding, of girls and young women aged 11–21, found that one in three feel under pressure to present themselves as having a 'perfect' life on social media.

It's easy to feel bad about ourselves for not being happy. And that just makes us feel worse. How come life is so rosy for other people? Maybe you think happiness is a matter of luck. It's not. Happiness is not a matter of coincidence or good luck. Neither, as Chapter 1 explains, is happiness a matter of living a blameless life or being in the right place at the right time. Happiness isn't given to you, you can't expect someone else to make you happy, you can't wait for the stars to align before you can be happy, and you can't just 'be happy'.

Quite simply, happiness is a matter of following your human instinct to find purpose and meaning, to manage the challenges that come with finding purpose and meaning, and to enjoy the small pleasures in life. This book – *Happiness* – will show you how to do that.

You will learn that happiness doesn't happen by chance – it's a result of the thought, time, and effort you put into pursuing and maintaining happiness. Happiness comes from identifying what's important in your life – in the different areas of your life: your work, your relationships, your hobbies and interests, your health, and so on – and having aims and purpose in those areas. Chapter 2 explains how you can identify and work towards what will make you happy (not what you think will make you happy or what other people think will make you happy).

Being happy – living according to your values, having goals, doing what is important to you and has meaning for you – not only involves making an effort and persevering, taking some risks and making sacrifices. It also means stepping out of your comfort zone. There will always be challenges and difficulties involved in pursuing happiness, but if you don't push yourself, nothing will change and you won't be happier. Chapter 3 explains how each time you extend your comfort zone you extend your happiness.

However, it could be that there's something you need to stop doing; something you need to let go of before you can commit and pursue the things or thing that would make you happy. Chapter 3 also has plenty of encouragement and advice on how to let go of unhappy situations and circumstances so you can move on to happier times.

Chapter 4 discusses the little things in life that can make you happy. Whatever your circumstances, whatever your abilities, however much money you do or don't have, there's a world of small pleasures which can bring you moments of happiness every day. Often, these small pleasures can be the things you do with other people.

Chapter 4 explains how almost anything we do to improve our connections with others tends to improve our happiness as well.

However, there will be times in all our lives when there are very real challenges to being happy; times when you're stuck in a situation – a job you dislike, for example – and you can see no way out. There are, though, things you can do to make the best out of a bad job. Chapter 5 explains what those things are.

How can you find any happiness when you've suffered or are suffering a serious difficulty? No doubt the last thing you can imagine is being happy. Chapter 5 discusses how you can find hope and therefore some happiness when life is really tough.

Having learnt how to find purpose and meaning in your life, and about the importance of identifying and indulging in small pleasures, connecting with other people, and knowing how to find some degree of happiness during difficult periods of your life, Chapter 6 looks at how you can help other people be happy. When someone you love and care about is unhappy, you feel it too; but whether you just want them to be happy so you can be happy, or you believe that you have the solutions to their problems, you cannot make it your mission to 'fix' them and make them happy. You can, though, be supportive. Chapter 6 explains how.

Why Be Happy?

Finally, just in case you need some encouragement to make the effort to pursue happiness, you might find it helpful to know what some of the benefits of happiness are. When you're living a happy life, you

- feel engaged with the world around you,
- have aims and goals that you can work towards and achieve,
- have good levels of confidence and positive self-esteem,
- build and maintain good relationships with others,
- more easily cope with the stresses of daily life,
- are more positive, more solution focused,
- manage better during difficult and challenging times in your life,
- help those around you to be happy.

With this book – *Happiness* – you will learn how to make happiness a habit. You will discover how to live a good life; a life that, despite its inevitable ups and downs, is both meaningful and pleasurable.

A happy life!

1
What Happiness Is

Happiness is not something you postpone for the future;
it is something you design for the present.

– Jim Rohn

We all think of happiness as something positive; something good that we want to feel and to be. But is it realistic to think we can be happy all the time? To answer this, it helps to understand that happiness happens in two ways: first as a long-term, general sense of wellbeing and second as a short-lived pleasure.

As a short-lived pleasure, happiness is a result of something that pleases us in some way – a funny joke, an uplifting film, a delicious meal, a good night out, a great holiday – and causes us to feel emotions such as contentment, satisfaction and enjoyment, delight, or joy. As a short-lived pleasure, this form of happiness is temporary; it's a passing happiness. Although short-lived pleasures do contribute towards happiness, we simply can't feel like this all the time. It's not realistic to think that we can.

But happiness is not only experienced as short-lived pleasure. We also experience happiness as a general sense of wellbeing. It's this sort of happiness – a general, stable sense of wellbeing, feeling fulfilled and feeling that life is good – that we can more realistically expect to experience if not all the time, then most of the time.

A Short History of Happiness

Although it might seem that everyone is in the pursuit of happiness nowadays, this is, in fact, nothing new. Over 2000 years ago, in his work 'Nicomachean Ethics' the Greek philosopher Aristotle explored the nature of the good life. He concluded that happiness – wellbeing – is a central purpose of human life; it's what we're all aiming for.

He identified the two types of happiness as *hedonic* happiness and *eudaimonic* happiness. Hedonic happiness is the small pleasures and eudaimonic happiness refers to a sense of meaning, purpose, and fulfilment.

Aristotle suggested that because, as human beings, we have a unique ability to reason – to use logic and good sense, to make judgements and come to conclusions – we should, indeed we must, use this ability to work out for ourselves ways to live our lives so that whatever else happens in life, we have a general, stable sense of wellbeing, feel fulfilled, and feel that, overall, life is good.

Aristotle acknowledged that happiness can be affected by such things as our health and wealth, friends, family, the work we do, where we live, etc. And yet, he said, by using our ability to think and reason, we are able to create a life for ourselves that enables us to bear the ups and downs of our existence with balance and perspective and maintain a general sense of wellbeing.

Fast forward 2000 years and, like Aristotle, today's psychologists and researchers are also interested in what makes for happiness and a good life. In his 2011 book *Flourish*, positive psychology professor, Martin Seligman, also suggests that in order to be happy we need to have one or more things in our life to aim for – things that mean something and make sense to us, that interest and absorb us, that we want to be involved in and allow us to feel good when we achieve what we set out to do. He says that, as social beings, we need to interact with others; to connect and feel that we belong. Seligman acknowledges that we need to experience short-lived pleasures in order to experience positive emotions such as contentment and enjoyment, inspiration, hope and joy, etc. But he recognises that although short-lived pleasures *contribute* to happiness, they are not the basis of happiness.

Of course, what's meaningful, engaging, and gives a sense of purpose is different for everyone. As is what makes for positive relationships and provides for positive emotions. But that's where the cognitive abilities that Aristotle referred to come in; we each need to work out for ourselves what makes for meaning and purpose, positive relationships, and small pleasures.

Aristotle and Seligman both agree that happiness requires thought and effort. This is a good thing! It means that the ability to be happy is within your power; *you* have the power to make yourself happy. You can discover for yourself what will bring sense and meaning to your life, what will engage and absorb you. You can identify what brings you pleasure – what the small things are in life that give you moments of happiness.

Rather than waiting to be happy, you can learn to be happy. You can make happiness a habit; your natural, normal way of being.

Unhelpful Beliefs

However, even if you can see that happiness *is* within your power, you may have beliefs and assumptions that have led you to conclude that happiness isn't possible for you.

In Chapter 3 we'll look at some of the obstacles that get in the way of being happy; we'll identify the potential problems, difficulties, and challenges and you'll read how to manage them. But first, let's look at some common, unhelpful beliefs about happiness.

I Don't Believe I Deserve to Be Happy

Maybe you feel you don't deserve happiness; you don't deserve to be happy because of something you did wrong in the past. You made the wrong decision to do or not do something. You blame yourself; you feel a sense of loss and sorrow and wish you could undo a choice that you made. Maybe you regret something you did or didn't do. Perhaps you did something that harmed or hurt someone else and now you feel guilty; you feel regret and remorse. You believe it would be wrong to try and be happy.

If that's the case, you need to know that regret, remorse, and guilt actually have a positive intent. Rather than keeping you stuck, the positive purpose of these 'negative' emotions is to prompt you to make up for your wrongdoing, to learn from your mistake and to behave differently in future.

Happy people learn from their mistakes and move on. You can do the same. Stop berating yourself for what you did wrong. Acknowledge and accept that what's done is done and can't be changed. There's nothing you can do about it. But what you *can* do is change what you do next.

It could be, though, that you haven't even done anything wrong. But you believe that you have. Perhaps you feel guilty that you can't alleviate someone's suffering, or that you didn't do enough to help someone. Perhaps you feel guilty that you survived something that other people did not. If that's the case, then you're experiencing imagined guilt. Imagined guilt happens when you feel guilty about events that, in fact, you were not, or are not, responsible for.

Maybe, for example, you feel that you can't appear to be happy while other people in your life are unhappy: your brother is unable to find a job or your partner is depressed; your sister is unable to conceive, a good friend's child died, or you received a promotion at the same time another friend was made redundant. But feeling undeserving doesn't help anyone. You haven't done anything wrong by being happy and showing that you're happy. If you're concerned about other people's situations, know that aiming for happiness is the right thing to do because then you're in a better position to help others to be happy. You can read more about how to help others be happy in Chapter 6.

I Don't Believe I Can Forgive

Perhaps, though, it's not that you feel *you've* done something wrong, it's that someone else has done you wrong and you can't move past that. Perhaps a friend has betrayed you, or your partner has had an affair, you've been unfairly sacked or you've suffered an injury as a result of someone else's actions. You don't believe you can be happy because you just can't forgive.

But forgiving doesn't mean giving in, minimising, excusing, or forgetting the offence; the other person is still responsible for their actions. They may not deserve to be forgiven for your pain, sadness, and suffering, but you deserve to be free of this negativity. Forgiveness is for you, not the other person. Forgiveness means letting go of the resentment, frustration, or anger that you feel as a result of someone else's actions. It involves no longer wanting punishment, revenge, or compensation. Acknowledge and accept that what's done is done and can't be changed. But what you can change is what you do next.

Life becomes easier when you learn to accept an apology you never got.

– Robert Brault

Of course, forgiveness is not a switch you can flip and then immediately forget what the other person did. But even if you don't have the will to forgive right now, you can still learn to live with the fact of the other person's wrongdoing as you work towards happiness.

I Don't Believe I Can Be as Happy as I Once Was

Maybe, though, it's not your own or someone else's wrongdoing in the past that holds you back from striving for happiness. Do you look back on other times and circumstances in your life and feel that everything was so much better then? Were you happier? There's nothing wrong with reminiscing – looking back on happy times in your life – but dwelling on those times can keep you stuck and deceive you into thinking you will never be that happy again.

You need to keep things in perspective. It's easy to idealise the past; to minimise, forget, or deliberately ignore difficulties that may also have occurred during the happier times. Even if you *were* able to recreate the same circumstances and situations when you were happier, it wouldn't be the same.

Whether the past really was that good or whether you've idealised it, dwelling on the past takes you away from making the most of the opportunities of the present. As someone once said: you can't start the next chapter of your life if you keep re-reading your last one.

I Don't Believe I Can Be as Happy as Other People
It could be that you believe that happiness is for other people. You compare yourself with them, see that they're happy and believe that your life can never be the same as theirs. You're right – it can't. Your life can't be the same as theirs. You are too unique to compare yourself fairly; your skills, abilities, contributions, and value are entirely unique to you and your purpose in this world. They can never be fairly compared to anyone else.

There will always be someone else you know, you hear about or read about in magazines and on social media to compare yourself to. There's always someone you can perceive as having more or doing better than you and therefore being happier than you.

But measuring your worth, your abilities, opportunities, your career progress, etc. against other people's can only lead to you feeling inferior. It's a sure-fire recipe for unhappiness. If you want to be happy you need to let go of comparing yourself to others. Jealousy and envy are incompatible with happiness, so if you're constantly comparing yourself to others, it's time to stop. Instead, be inspired by others and, with the help of this book, start planning how you can work towards what you want. This will make you more positive and in control, since you are no longer looking at what the other person has that you haven't – you'll be too busy working towards what you want. You won't have the time or a reason to be envious!

I Don't Believe I Can Be Happy Until Something Changes in My Life

Are you waiting for something to happen before you can be happy? Do you believe that you'll only be happy once your perfect partner comes along, or the perfect job or new home materialises? Maybe you're waiting for a relationship to end, the neighbours to move, or someone to die. Perhaps you're waiting to have a baby or for the children to leave home. Or it could be that you believe you can only be happy once you're healthier, you've lost weight, or got fitter.

It's easy to believe that happiness is something you'll achieve once all the stars have aligned and something else in your life is finally in place. But this is just a story you've been telling yourself. Happiness is not circumstantial. And that's actually good news; you don't have to wait for everything to be perfect. Instead, you can learn to be happy while you're waiting for that big lottery win, the perfect partner, the perfect job, or whatever it is you're hoping for. When it comes to happiness, the journey is just as important as the destination; the journey is an inherent part of happiness.

In a Nutshell

- Happiness happens in two ways: first as a long-term, general sense of wellbeing – *eudaimonic* happiness; and second as a short-lived pleasure – *hedonic* happiness.
- Aristotle suggests that, using our ability to think and reason, we can – indeed we must – each work out for ourselves what makes for meaning, purpose, and small pleasures in our lives.
- The fact that happiness requires you to give it your thought and effort is a good thing! It means that the ability to be happy is within your power; you have the power to make yourself happy.
- Rather than waiting to be happy, you can learn to be happy. You can make happiness a habit; your natural, normal way of being.
- However, you may have beliefs and assumptions that have led you to conclude that happiness isn't possible for you.
- Maybe you feel you don't deserve to be happy because of something you did wrong in the past. What's done is done and whatever you did wrong can't be changed. But what you can change is what you do next.

- If you're experiencing imagined guilt, you feel guilty for events that, actually, you were not responsible for. And if you're concerned about other people's situations, know that being happy is the right thing to be because then you're in a better position to help others to be happy.
- Even if you don't have the will to forgive someone's wrongdoing towards you right now, you can still learn to live with the fact of the other person's wrongdoing as you work towards happiness.
- If you don't believe you can be as happy as you once were, know that whether the past really was that good or whether you've idealised it, dwelling on it takes you away from making the most of the opportunities of the present.
- Jealousy and envy are incompatible with happiness. Instead of comparing your situation and yourself with others, be inspired by them. Start planning how you can work towards what you want and be happy.
- You don't have to wait for something in your life to be in place, for the stars to have aligned and everything to be perfect, before you can start being happy. Instead, you can learn to be happy while you're waiting for whatever it is you're hoping for.

2

How to Be Happy: Find Purpose and Meaning

Know What's Important to You; Know Your Values

Your values become your destiny.

– Mahatma Gandhi

To be happy, then, you need meaning and purpose in your life; but how do you find meaning and purpose?

In order to stand any chance of finding meaning and purpose we need to first understand what's important to us; we need to start with our values.

We all have values and we each have different values. Maybe you've not given much thought to what your values are, but that doesn't mean you don't have them. Quite simply, your values are those things that are important to you and give weight to the way that you live, work, and relate to other people.

What have your values got to do with being happy? In different areas of your life, when what you do and how you live matches your values, things will just feel right. What you do and how you live will feel compatible with what's important to you. And that will help you to be happy.

As we grow up, we learn values, morals, and rules for the 'right' and 'wrong' way to be and behave from our parents, family and friends, our school, community, and culture. It's likely that the values you internalised as a child will have remained with you through adulthood. Core values such as truth and honesty, kindness and fairness are, of course, always admirable and worthwhile. However, other values that you may have been brought up with – ambition and achievement, success, excellence, and perfection – may not have proved important to you; maybe the values of spontaneity and adventure, risk, and courage were more appealing.

Or, it could be that you were brought up in a family or culture where the values of self-discipline, self-reliance, persistence, duty, and respect were paramount. Although you haven't totally rejected those values, your priorities are more in line with the values of empathy, belonging, care, and kindness. Or perhaps creativity, the pursuit of beauty, harmony, and peace are more important to you.

What core values were you raised with? What did your parents value and what values did they impress upon you? What values were reflected in the way you were rewarded or disciplined? Are your current values the same as those you grew up with? Have you consciously dropped some values from your upbringing and adopted different ones?

Usually, adolescence is a time when – in your efforts to forge your own individual identity (who you are) and your social identity (how you fit in with others) – you question and reject some or even all of the values you were brought up with and establish your own. But maybe you've never questioned the values you were brought up with; you've simply accepted them and created your life around those values. That's all well and good if you're happy, but if you're living your life or parts of your life according to values that you don't really believe in, you may well feel conflicted, out of balance, and unhappy.

It's not just the values your parents impressed upon you that have an impact; the values of your culture and society have a strong influence too. The pursuit of wealth and material goods, academic qualifications, status and power, winning, being popular, and attractive have become dominant values in much of Western society.

Too often, too many of us subscribe to these values in the mistaken belief that they are the only route to happiness and success.

You don't have to make your life look like anybody else says it should look.

– Dee Rees

Mike Lewis is the author of a book called *When to Jump*. In the book, he describes how, at the age of 23, he landed his dream job at Bain, a venture capital investment firm. The job was interesting, he had a good boss and got on with his colleagues. Mike had taken the job at Bain because of a genuine, enthusiastic interest in the work. His parents were right behind him. 'But', he writes, 'I had somehow got it into my head that I was supposed to stick to a certain path and the job at Bain fitted into that kind of path; from college to internship to a well-paying corporate job. At Bain I was on the "right" path, surrounded by smart people, doing interesting work and enjoying well-paid vacations. What else could I want? Yet deep down, as time went by, I began to realise that I wanted this life mostly because I thought I should. And all the while, tucked somewhere off to the side of my mind, a very distinct if faint voice whispered an idea of something very different. I was in love with the sport of squash.'

If, rather than pursuing your own values and doing what you think is important, you're living a life that's dictated by others – according to values that are not truly yours – it's a struggle to be happy because you're going down the wrong path; you're going in a direction that takes you away from what's important to you; what really makes sense and has meaning to you.

No doubt you'll have heard the exhortation to 'be true to yourself' and may have wondered, as I used to, what exactly that means; how can you be true to yourself? Well, when you're living your life in ways that are in line with your values, when you're doing what's important to you – not what you think you 'should' be doing or what other people think is important – then you're being true to yourself. You're being real, genuine, and authentic. Admittedly, being true to yourself will present challenges and difficulties, but, ultimately, you're living your life in a way that reflects who and what you really want to be.

Bronnie Ware spent several years working in palliative care in Australia, caring for patients in the last weeks of their lives. She talked with her patients and listened to them as they looked back over their past. As a result of these conversations, in 2012 Bronnie published a book: *The Top Five Regrets of the Dying*.

The top regret that people expressed? 'I wish I'd had the courage to live a life true to myself, not the life others expected of me.'

The first thing that stops many people from living a life that's true to them is the fact that they haven't actually identified *what* is true to them; they haven't clarified what their values are; what's meaningful and important to them. So, identifying your own values is the first step towards living your own life; living a life that's true to you.

Identify Your Core Values

What are your values? To help you identify these, here is a list of some common core values. Tick any that are important to you. Add any you think of that are not included on the list.

Accountability	Control
Achievement	Cooperation
Adventure	Courage
Affection	Courtesy
Altruism	Creativity
Ambition	Curiosity
Amusement	Decisiveness
Appreciation	Dependability
Approachability	Determination
Approval	Dignity
Balance	Directness
Beauty	Discipline
Belonging	Discretion
Calmness	Duty
Care	Empathy
Certainty	Enjoyment
Clarity	Equality
Commitment	Excellence
Compassion	Excitement
Confidence	Fairness
Connection	Family
Consistency	Fidelity
Continuity	Freedom of speech
Contributing	Frugality

Fun	Professionalism
Generosity	Punctuality
Gratitude	Reliability
Harmony	Respect
Honesty	Security
Humility	Self-control
Independence	Self-reliance
Integrity	Simplicity
Intimacy	Sincerity
Justice	Spirituality
Kindness	Spontaneity
Loyalty	Stability
Open-mindedness	Structure
Optimism	Success
Peace	Support
Perfection	Trust
Persistence	Truth
Popularity	Understanding
Privacy	Unity

Once you've been through them, narrow down your list to between five and seven values. These are your 'core' values; your most important, essential values.

Some of your values are likely to be personal values: values that are concerned with how you behave and respond to situations; values such as optimism, clarity, privacy, or security. You will probably also have social values – values such as compassion, fairness and coop- eration, reliability, or honesty – which concern the way you interact with other people. You may have more personal values than social values. You may have more social values than personal values. It doesn't matter – whatever your values, they are what is important to *you*.

Interpret and Better Understand Your Values

Once you've identified your core values, give some thought to what each of those values means to you. Different values mean different things to different people, so it's useful to define what each value means to you and how it relates to your life.

You might find it helpful to write it down. The process of defining, in writing, what each value means to you can help you further clarify what it is and why it's important to you. For each value, answer these questions:

- What does the word (the value) mean? What does the dictionary say this word means? (Look it up on www.dictionary.com.) Do I agree with that definition? How would I describe to someone else what this word means to me, how it applies to my life?
- Why is this value important to me?
- In what way is this value currently a part of my life? How do I live this value? If, for example, kindness and compassion were my values, how, where, and when am I able to be kind and compassionate?
- Do I need more opportunities in my life to live my core values?

Secondary Values and Goals

As well as core values, you also have secondary values. Secondary values are those things that are important to you in a specific area or aspect of your life. Your work, for example, is an area of your life and so you will have work values: beliefs about what's important to you in a job. Your relationships with your partner, family, and friends are other areas or aspects of your life. So you will have relationship values: ideas and beliefs about what's important to you in a friendship or relationship with a partner or other family member.

Knowing your core values and secondary values in different areas of your life can help you find meaning and purpose; help you to identify goals and have things to work towards and aim for.

Below, you will read about how all the areas of your life – friendships and relationships, health, work, finances, your home, hobbies, and interests – have the potential for you to create sense, meaning, and purpose; to have aims and goals. Of course, identifying values and goals is just the first step. The next steps are to work out ways to pursue the goals and then ways to manage the challenges that will inevitably arise. More about that later in this chapter!

Work and Career

To be happy, you need to live a life that is in harmony with your values and, if you work, then your work is a large part of your life. Between 2011 and 2012, the polling and management consulting firm Gallup conducted a detailed study looking at how people felt about their work. Only 13% of people said they were 'engaged' in their work; that they found it meaningful and looked forward to it. Most people, instead, were unhappy in their jobs. In fact, two-thirds were 'not engaged' at work, they felt no real connection to their jobs or, worse, they resented their jobs.

When you enjoy your work and you're engaged in what you're doing, you're using your skills and strengths. And, just as importantly, your work should relate to your values.

In a newspaper interview, Anita Roddick, founder of the beauty products company The Body Shop, said: 'I've never been able to separate Body Shop values from my own core values; values of optimism, fun, caring, family, and community'. And later, on her website, she wrote, 'It is impossible to separate the company values from the issues that I care passionately about – social responsibility, respect for human rights, the environment and animal protection, and an absolute belief in Community Trade.'

Does your work or career reflect your core values? Does your job reflect your work values? Your work values are the secondary values – things that are important to you in a job, work, or career – which, along with core values, help give purpose and meaning to your work.

Perhaps the work you do or the career you're involved in is more a reflection of what someone else – your teachers or parents, for example – told you was important in a job or career. For example, if your parents held qualifications, status, and high earnings among their work values, it's more than likely that they impressed those values on you too. But what if you don't share the same values and, right now, you would rather be selling ice cream on a beach in the south of France? Or perhaps you aspire to be a tree surgeon rather than a heart surgeon. You want to be a tattoo artist, not a fine artist.

I recently asked a couple of friends, both in their 50s and both of whom run their own business, what they thought would make them happier in their work. They were both quite clear that at this stage in their life, it would be to earn more money but work fewer hours. Is that important to you – could that be a goal for you, too? Or do you have different work values and goals?

Perhaps job security or promotion opportunities are important to you. Maybe it's having authority, leadership and influence, prestige, and high pay. Perhaps flexible hours, low levels of responsibility, being shown appreciation, and a pleasant environment are important for you in a job. Or maybe a job where no two days are the same is important to you – you like to be involved in a variety of tasks and activities. Maybe it is important to you to be involved with work that's practical, creative, or inventive. Or you like to be able to work on your own; be autonomous and make all your own decisions.

What are your work values? Is there something missing in your job, work, or career – something that is important to you – around which you could create some goals; some work-related goals?

Perhaps you realise that in order to be doing something that more closely matches your core values and your work values, you really need to change your career, to re-train or work freelance, or run your own business. Maybe you want to work abroad or return to full-time study.

It could be that you simply want to change some aspects of your job – work flexible hours or have a wider range of tasks and responsibilities or more challenging work. Maybe you want to develop your skills or qualifications in your current profession.

What's of importance to you in your job, your work or career? What, if anything, do you think would make you happier in your work? What could you aim for; what work-related goals might you have?

Finances

Could you have some goals related to your finances? Maybe you want to start saving or save more. Maybe it's important that you save up money for an emergency fund. Perhaps you want to invest some or get a mortgage. Maybe you want to organise life insurance or a pension. Perhaps you simply want to earn more. Perhaps you'd like to pay off your mortgage early, or it could be that being debt free has become important to you; you want to pay off your debts – your credit card debts, for example.

Your Home

Whether you rent or own, whether you plan to be there for three more months, three more years, or thirty years, you may have things that you want to get done in your home. You might want to refurbish, furnish, redecorate, make some repairs, or simply declutter your home. Perhaps you're thinking about getting a cleaner.

Health

What does good health mean to you? What are your health values: what's important to you when it comes to being in good health? If you've no health problems, you might take it for granted and give it no thought or make no effort to maintain your good health.

For someone else, though, maintaining good health might involve eating healthy foods, going to the gym and yoga classes, and getting enough sleep. For others, good health means making sure they stay on top of a chronic health condition they are suffering from – taking their medication, doing physio exercises, and having regular health checks.

You might want to think about setting some goals related to your physical health. Maybe you want to lose weight, stop smoking, build more exercise into your life, do some strength training, take up running, or simply be able to walk up three flights of stairs without being out of breath.

It could be that you set goals related to your mental health; maybe, for example, you've been struggling with depression or anxiety and you want to set some goals around managing that.

In 2017, in an article for The Pool (www.the-pool.com), author Marie Phillips experienced what she described as 'a mini burnout'. 'I was miserable all the time, lacking in energy, unwilling to see friends and unable to work. I tried and tried to feel happier, forcing myself to soldier on and put on a smiling face. Nothing worked … I decided that I wasn't going to try to feel happy any more. I decided that I needed to look after myself better, not in order to be happy, but to stop myself from getting so overwhelmed in the future.'

Marie decided to take better care of her physical and mental health. Among other things, she said: 'I've improved my diet (less meat, more veg); I limit myself to no more than two alcoholic drinks per night (this is the thing I've done that has had the single largest impact on my anxiety); I take more exercise (walking or cycling every day, plus I've taken up rowing); I meditate daily ... I found a life coach who taught me, amongst other things, to have better boundaries; I stopped reading the news because it was killing me with stress; I turn down work I really don't want to do even if it's well paid ... and I've rearranged my living arrangements with my boyfriend so that I can work from home.'

Marie wrote that 'The key thing, though, is that none of it is aimed at turning me into a happy person,' but, she admitted, after six months of healthy living, she did feel much happier.

'By focusing on being healthy, I've crept up on happiness from the side – I feel calm and rested; I'm enjoying work again; I'm more present as a partner and a friend. Perhaps all along I already had what I needed in my life to feel happy, but only in working on my health did I become well enough to appreciate it.'

Marie is probably right; all along she *did* already have what she needed in her life to feel happy. But it was once she recognised what was important to her – her health – and she created goals related to her health that, without realising it, she created the meaning and purpose she needed to be happier.

As the philosopher A.C. Grayling says: 'Happiness comes as a sideline of other endeavours that, in themselves, bring satisfaction and a sense of achievement.'

Friends and Family

So many studies have shown that friendships boost our happiness. In 2002, Professors Ed Diener and Martin Seligman, for example, conducted a study at the University of Illinois which showed that a person's happiness is highly correlated with social relationships. They reported that: 'The most salient characteristics shared by the 10% of students with the highest levels of happiness and the fewest signs of depression were their strong ties to friends and family and commitment to spending time with them.'

What's important to you in a friendship and in your relationships with family members? Perhaps having fun and lots of laughs together is what's important to you. Perhaps it's simply to have one or more shared interests. Certainly, having shared interests, shared experiences, and a shared history creates connections and bonds between people. But while sharing the same interests – a love of Hip Hop music and a passion for football – might be important to some people in a friendship, it could be that, for you, shared interests aren't a priority – mutual support, care, and concern are more important aspects of a friendship.

Think about what's important to you in a friendship. Could you improve your friendships and relationships with others? In what way?

It could be that you want to make more time to spend with your friends, family, or partner. Just hang out together or do some fun, interesting things together; go to gigs, join a choir, learn a new skill together, maybe have a weekend away or a holiday together.

Perhaps you're aiming to organise something special for a friend; a birthday treat. Perhaps you want to be able to spend more time supporting a friend or family member who's going through a difficult time. Or you want to make amends over something you fell out over.

Which of your friends do you want to spend more time with? Have you even got the friends you want? Are you happy with the friends you have? Do you want more like-minded friends? Maybe you feel you have very few or no friends at all and you'd simply like to make some friends.

Think about what, if anything, you could do to create more meaningful friendships and relationships.

Interests and Hobbies

How about creating some meaning and purpose by taking up a new hobby or broadening your skills and knowledge in an area that interests you?

Perhaps there's something you'd like to learn – something creative or practical or something that's simply just fun. Perhaps you'd like to play a musical instrument or learn a language. Maybe learning to sail, to ride a horse, to dance a waltz, or to master five magic tricks interests you.

Is there something you can already do that you'd like to get better at; your ability to speak another language, for example, or to play the guitar or to cook? Perhaps being creative is important to you; you'd like to paint or draw, take photos, make pottery, or design and sew your own clothes.

Perhaps you want to travel; visit Rome or Rio de Janeiro, Tahiti, Tibet or Turkey or see the Taj Mahal, hike along The Great Wall of China or the Grand Canyon.

Maybe you could have goals related to your personal development; to be more confident or assertive, for example. You may want to develop your spirituality; if a strong sense of connection and belonging – of being part of something bigger, more eternal than yourself – is important to you, then you could explore ways you could fulfil that value. Although your spiritual needs might be realised by being part of an organised religion, you could discover instead that this comes from being part of a group – a choir or an orchestra, or as a supporter of a national sports team, or a global organisation such as Amnesty International. You might aim to develop your spirituality by connecting with nature, through an activity such as gardening, hiking, fishing, sailing, or simply gazing at the stars.

Voluntary Work

We are all here on earth to help others; what on earth the others are here for I don't know.

– W.H. Auden

For many people, their core values include caring, compassion, altruism, and contributing and so a key way to create meaning and purpose in their lives is through their involvement in and contribution to other people's lives; helping and supporting others – helping to improve their local community, for example, or being involved with a local, national, or international cause, or a pressure group.

Here's Carla's story: Carla worked for an accountancy company. She was highly paid and enjoyed her work; it provided all the things that were important to her in a job – authority and responsibility, reliability, accountability, control – but in the last year Carla felt that something was missing.

Although her work values hadn't changed – her job continued to be enjoyable and engage her – Carla had another set of values – social values – that weren't being fulfilled by her work. Carla wanted to be doing something that would enable her to make a positive difference to other people's lives; she wanted to be involved in contributing to other people's lives in a fun, active way.

Carla remembered how much she'd enjoyed being in the Girl Guides when she was a teenager, so she got in contact to find out what opportunities there might be for her to get involved as an adult. She was invited to train to be a Unit Leader, responsible for setting up and running a local Girl Guides group, leading a team, planning and taking part in a programme of fun activities and events. Within a few months, among other activities, Carla had organised and led a kayaking weekend for a group of teenage girls.

If you're interested in volunteering your time and skills, there's a huge range of volunteer opportunities available to you. Whether it's serving tea at a local hospice, helping at a local community food project or an animal rescue centre, working with refugees, advocating for someone with a learning disability or mental health problem, or mentoring people leaving the criminal justice system, not only can you make a contribution to other people's lives, but you can be involved in something that's relevant to your values and interests. It could be something related to politics, the environment and conservation, arts and music, or perhaps some voluntary work with older people, families, or children.

When you do something to benefit others, you not only help them but you also know you're making a positive contribution and doing good; there's real purpose, sense and meaning.

Happiness Habit: Review Your Values

Every now and again, review your values; your core values and your secondary values. Nothing in life remains the same; what is important to you in a job or in a friendship may not be the same today as it was a few years ago. Be aware that your values may change according to changes in your life. Be prepared, also, to modify your values according to different circumstances.

Identifying and Working Towards Goals

We each have different aspects to our lives – family, friends, and our social life, work, health, hobbies and interests, spirituality, and so on – in which we have values and we can have goals related to those values. Thinking about what your values are – thinking about what's important to you in each area of your life – can help you to set goals. Setting goals helps you to see that you have choices, and that you have control and that you can make progress and achieve.

The aim isn't to have lots and lots of goals, it's simply to be aware that you do have these different areas of your life and each area has values and the potential for goals that can provide purpose and meaning. In other words, each area has the potential to contribute towards your overall happiness.

So, having started to think about the different areas of your life – what's important to you in each area and what might improve each area and help you to be happier – the next step is to have some specific goals to work towards.

When you set goals, you give yourself something specific to work towards; you create for yourself a sense of meaning and purpose – a positive path to follow. The path won't always run smoothly or be easy (we'll look at how to deal with that later in this chapter), but having goals will point you in the direction you want to go and engage you in the things that are important to you. And that's all good for your overall happiness!

Your goals can be as big as starting a charity or building your own house, or as simple as growing herbs in a window box or being able to wear high-heeled shoes out in public. (Seriously. Earlier today a young woman – Gemma – told me that this is one of her goals.) The crucial thing is that you identify and have things to work on, make progress on, and look forward to achieving.

There's a process involved. You'll need to think about and identify:

1. The specific goal: be clear about what you want to achieve.
2. The benefits: know why it is important to you; what you'll gain from achieving your goal.

3. Your options: the different ways you could work towards your goal.
4. The steps: each step you'll need to take in order to achieve your goal.

Identify the Goal

Identify some thing or things you'd like to do that you can work towards and achieve in an area or areas of your life. They could be short-term goals – things you want to achieve in the next few weeks or months; or longer-term goals – things you want to achieve in the next year or years in your life.

You may come up with one or two goals or you might come up with several. How many you can work on at any one time depends on what else you've got going on in your life already; the commitments you already have.

You can't, though, rely on just one thing in your life to make you happy. That's putting all your eggs into one basket. Happy people know that they need to have happiness in different areas of their lives so that if one aspect of their life becomes difficult and unhappy, they have happiness in other parts of their life that supports them through.

You could find there's some overlap; that a goal in one area extends to another aspect of your life. For example, if you wanted to get more fit and healthy and you also wanted to spend more time with one of your friends, you might find an activity you could regularly do together – for example, swimming or hiking, going to the gym, or dance classes.

Identify the Benefits

Why is a particular goal important to you? In what way will you benefit from achieving your goal? Although, to some extent, you may feel that a particular goal presents a challenge, first and foremost your goals should inspire you. It's not difficult to be inspired; you simply need to identify the benefits – what you stand to gain from working towards and achieving each goal. Knowing the benefits of achieving your goal can also help keep you motivated when you come across any obstacles and problems.

Identify Your Options

For each goal, you'll need to think through how it could be achieved. What skills, strengths, and resources do you have that could help you? What further information do you need? What advice or help might you need? Who could help you?

If, for example, one of your goals is to learn something new or improve a skill you already have (and learning is an obvious way to see yourself making progress with something), think about *how* you might learn. Is there a course local to you? Could you hire a private tutor, or ask a friend or colleague to teach you? Could you learn from a book or sign up to an online course? Are there any YouTube tutorials that you could watch?

Weigh up the pros and cons of each option. Think about how you feel about each. If you feel inspired, it's the right choice.

Gemma thought that she could just walk to the local shops in her high heels or she could wear them to the pub that evening, but she decided her best option was to wear her high-heeled shoes to the supermarket the next day. She told me she figured she'd then have the support of the shopping trolley as she tottered around the supermarket!

Here's another example of someone – Joe – identifying their options: 'Three years ago I landed a great freelance job in the film industry. It was exciting and glamorous. Everyone was really cool and fun. I started buying expensive clothes – designer outfits. I constantly went out to clubs and restaurants with my new colleagues. I spent money like water.

I was renting a flat on my own and the bills started mounting up and I got into debt. I realised that I needed to get a grip. My goal was to be debt free and stay that way.

I sat down and wrote out what my options were. I could:

- Fix my debts with one big consolidation loan, with a three-year repayment term.
- Work a couple of shifts in a pub at the weekend.
- Get a lodger.

- Stop using Uber and Deliveroo and cancel my gym membership. I could buy a secondhand bike and ride it everywhere. I could swap eating out for inviting friends round to my place for pasta and cheap plonk. Instead of holidays abroad, I could visit family and friends in Devon and Scotland.

Once I had written down my goal and options, I felt a huge sense of relief. I also felt I had regained some control. Even if there were setbacks, I still felt it was going to be possible to be debt-free at some point in the future. Identifying my goals and options gave me the belief that things could improve for the better. I felt hopeful and a lot happier.'

Identify the Steps

Whatever goals you have, the way to make sure things aren't too hard or difficult is for a goal to be broken down into smaller, more doable steps. Taking a step-by-step approach means you set yourself up for constant success by achieving small targets along the way. That means small shots of happiness each time you achieve each step.

So, work out all the steps you think you need to take towards your goal. Just empty your mind; you don't need to write things down in any particular order just yet. If, for example, you wanted to change career direction, the things you'd need to do could include talking to a careers advisor or coach, spending time online researching jobs and training in the career you're interested in, and re-writing your CV. These are all part of the larger goal, but breaking them down makes them easier to think about and to work on.

Now, out of all the steps involved in your goal, decide what the first one will be. And then, what will be the next?

Each step may or may not be challenging in some way. If it feels overwhelming or too difficult, break that step down into a few smaller steps.

By setting goals for yourself you give yourself something to aim for. But, contrary to what you might think, you don't have to wait until you've achieved your goals – until you've got the job or career, the friends, the home, the lifestyle, or whatever it is you're aiming for – before you can be happy. Happiness comes from working towards your goals. The steps you take towards each goal let you see yourself consistently making progress. And progress equals happiness. It's like reading a good book – you don't read a book just to find out what happens at the end, you read it to enjoy each chapter. (Don't you?)

> ## Happiness Habit: Keep your Mind Focused on One Step at a Time
>
> Tell yourself 'this is what I'm going to do next' and then just focus on that one step you're taking. Set yourself up for constant successes by achieving small targets along the way and you will see yourself moving forward.

You might be concerned about the time it is going to take to achieve what you want; you worry that if, for example, you start to learn a new skill, it could take months, even years, to perfect it. Or, if you want to move to the country, it might be a long time before the right place comes up. Instead of thinking about how long it will take, know that a step-by-step plan allows you to simply work consistently towards what it is you want to achieve, however long it takes.

Imagine, for example, that one of your goals was to declutter your home. It's unlikely you'll do it all in one go. Instead, you might decide to do a different room each weekend. You'll probably break it down further so that you sort out one cupboard, or one shelf, or one type of thing – books or clothes, for example – at a time.

It might not be easy; you might come across problems along the way – trying to decide what to keep and what not to keep, what to do with what you no longer want – but, and this is the crucial thing, each stage you complete is a small goal in itself. Each drawer you clear out is a small achievement. And, if you make a point of reflecting on each small achievement and feeling pleased with yourself, then each of those small achievements will help you feel happy!

Doing things one step at a time gives you time to look at what is working and what isn't, and to decide if you need to change anything. So, as you go through each step, review the outcome. What's worked? What helped and went well?

Manage the Difficulties and Setbacks

It is the supple tree which bends in the gale while the one that is stiff and rigid either snaps or is pulled up by the roots.

– Ursula Markham

It's likely that as you work towards any one goal, problems will arise. Life will always have something unexpected to throw your way, which is something we can all expect. So, you'll need to be flexible and prepared to change course in light of the unexpected!

Suppose you were planning a journey; maybe you're going to drive somewhere 200 miles away. You've looked at your options – the different routes you could take to get there. You've decided what the best route is and you set off. All's going well but after 50 miles there's a traffic jam and they've closed the road ahead. Or you get a puncture. Or maybe the motorway service station you planned to stop at for a meal is closed. What to do? Do you give up? Of course you don't. You identify and assess your options and you decide what you're going to do next.

It's the same approach with setbacks to anything you set out to do – you identify what, exactly, the problem is and then you look for a solution. You might be able to deal with the problem or you might conclude that Plan A isn't, after all, going to work out. So, you switch to Plan B.

If, when you were thinking through how to achieve your goal, you identified some alternative options for achieving that goal, you will have already identified a Plan B.

Whether it's travel plans, a change of career, getting fit, or improving a relationship with a friend or family member, things happen. The weather changes, a road is closed, someone you were relying on drops out, you fall or sustain an injury, it costs more money than you expected. But, if you really want it, there's always a way. And, most likely, there's more than one way. As someone once said: 'If Plan A doesn't work, the alphabet has 25 more letters.'

Plan for Difficulties

In fact, when you're planning how to achieve a goal, you can anticipate potential problems and possible solutions. For each step, think about what could go wrong. What's the worst that could happen?

Thinking like this is not designed to discourage you and put you off doing what you want to do. It's making it more likely you'll be successful. How come? Because you've anticipated the potential problems and you've already thought through how you would deal with them. Forewarned is forearmed!

What will you do if you run out of time, money or the ability to do something? Perhaps you're keen to take on a new project at work or you want to work freelance or start a business. What might the potential problems be? Think through how you could deal with them. Who could help? What support, advice, finances, or resources could you draw on?

Happiness Habit: Learn from Difficulties

If or when things don't go to plan, when there are problems and setbacks, as well as identifying your options and finding solutions, ask yourself 'what can I learn from this'? and 'what will I do differently, now'? Focus on learning and improving. Focus on what can be done rather than what can't be done; be open to new ideas and new ways of doing things.

Happiness Habit: Keep Motivated

Remind yourself of a good reason for pursuing your goal; why it's important to you. What will the benefits be of achieving what you want? Maybe it's a financial or material gain. Perhaps it's personal gain: you'll learn something new, be healthier or improve yourself or your situation in some way. Maybe it's related to your social values – that you'll be making a positive contribution to other people's lives. Whatever it is, get into the habit of reminding yourself how pursuing and achieving your goal will improve your life.

Happiness Habit: Reach Out for Support and Encouragement

In Chapter 1 you will have read that Professor Martin Seligman suggests that in order to be happy, as well as having aims and goals, we need positive relationships; we need to connect and interact with others. One reason for connecting with others is the advice and information, support, and encouragement we can get from other people; from friends, family, colleagues, or professionals. So, share your goals with other people. As Karl Marx advises: 'Surround yourself with people who make you happy. People who make you laugh, who help you when you're in need. People who genuinely care. They are the ones worth keeping in your life. Everyone else is just passing through.'

Happiness Habit: Review Progress

Take stock of your progress – of what you've achieved – on a regular basis. No matter how slow things seem, if you're working towards the next step, then you're making progress!

Happiness Habit: Remain Flexible

Be prepared to modify your goals. Your priorities and your goals may well change as time goes on, so adjust them to reflect new knowledge and experience. And if a specific goal no longer feels appropriate, then let it go. A few years ago, for example, I started a Masters degree in Education with the Open University. Although it was interesting, after the first module, I changed my mind about continuing. I altered my goal: rather than pay to do research and write, I decided to find a way to be paid to research and write. And that's how come I wrote my first book.

And Finally

If you're wondering about Mike and Gemma, Mike resigned from his job at the venture capital firm and spent two years following his dream of being a professional squash player. It meant, he says, 'living on sofas, mostly broke but feeling fulfilled'. Gemma wore her high-heeled shoes round the supermarket that evening. She told me it was an achievement for her – it made her happy!

In a Nutshell

- In different areas of your life, when what you do and how you live matches your values, things will just feel right. What you do and how you live will feel compatible with what's important to you. And that will help you to be happy.

(Continued)

(*Continued*)

- But if you're living your life or parts of your life according to values that you don't really believe in, you may well feel conflicted, out of balance, and unhappy.
- Knowing your core values and secondary values in different areas of your life can help you find meaning and purpose, help you to identify goals and have things to work towards and aim for.
- The aim isn't to have lots and lots of goals, it's simply to be aware that you do have these different areas of your life – work, friends and family, health, hobbies, and interests, etc. – and each area has values and the potential for goals that provide purpose and meaning and can contribute towards your overall happiness.
- As the philosopher A.C. Grayling says: 'Happiness comes as a sideline of other endeavours that, in themselves, bring satisfaction and a sense of achievement.'
- There's a process involved; you'll need to think about and identify the specific goal, what you'll gain from achieving your goal, the options for working towards your goal, and what steps you'll need to take in order to achieve your goal.
- When you're planning how to achieve a goal, think about what could go wrong. Anticipating potential problems makes it more likely you'll be able to deal with them because you've already thought them through. So, think who could help. What support, advice, finances, or resources could you draw on?

Happiness Habits

- If, or when, there are problems and setbacks, as well as finding solutions, learn from difficulties.
- Remind yourself regularly of the good reasons for pursuing and achieving your goal.
- Get advice and support from other people.
- Regularly review your progress as you work towards your goal and note what you've achieved so far.
- Regularly review and, if necessary, modify or change your goals.

3

Step Out of Your Comfort Zone

Your life does not get better by chance. It gets better by change.

– Jim Rohn

Whatever it is you want to do, whatever goals you'd like to achieve, despite your good intentions you might think 'it'll take too long to achieve' or 'it's going to be too hard' or 'it's too late'. It could be that you think 'I don't have the skills or ability', 'I might not do it right', 'my friends might not like it', or 'my family will disapprove'. It's true; it might be too hard, it might be too late, other people might not like it or disapprove.

There will always be challenges and difficulties. But if you stay where you are, if you don't push yourself, nothing will change and you won't be happier.

Step Out of Your Comfort Zone

What would you do if you knew it wasn't too late? What would you do if you had the skills, knowledge, and ability to achieve what you want? What would you do if you weren't worried about other people's reactions? What would you do if you were sure it would definitely turn out well?

Too often, there's something you'd like to do but because you know it's going to take some effort and there's going to be some difficulties, you stay where you are; you stay in the same boring job or career, for example, sticking with the course that you really don't like, or putting up with unsatisfactory friendships and relationships. You believe it's safer not to make changes, not to try new experiences or learn new things.

Although you may be dissatisfied and frustrated, although you may not be happy or feel fulfilled, it's been like this – you've had these routines and commitments, this job or career, these relationships and friendships – for months or years. It's what you know, so you might as well stick with it.

Palliative care nurse Bronnie Ware found that many of the people she spoke to at the end of their lives recognised that for much of their time they had stayed stuck in old patterns and habits. And they regretted it. She says: 'The so-called "comfort" of familiarity overflowed into their ... lives. Fear of change had them pretending to others, and to their selves, that they were content.'

Don't be one of those people!

Don't, for example, be like Ali. Ali figured that if he didn't try, if he didn't take any risks in life, then he couldn't fail. Although he really wanted a partner, one special person to share his life with – someone to share interests with, someone who might love him and care about him – Ali wasn't prepared to widen his social life; to meet new people and to accept invitations to things he wouldn't normally have gone to. He felt that it might not be worth the time and effort. He certainly wasn't going to try internet dating or go on any of the blind dates that his friend wanted to set him up with; what if the other person was boring or stupid? Or what if he liked the other person but they weren't interested in him? Better to turn down a date than accept it and the other person not call him again.

This was Ali's approach to most things in life – he took no risks. While this approach kept Ali 'safe' it also meant that he rarely got what he wanted in life. By risking nothing – by staying in his comfort zone – Ali was trapped in his limited life. He was not happy.

You can't change situations you don't take responsibility for. Sigmund Freud once said: 'Most people do not really want freedom, because freedom involves responsibility, and most people are frightened of responsibility.'

It's the same with happiness – most people don't want happiness, because happiness involves responsibility.

If you're like Ali, the more you avoid making changes, the more entrenched in old habits and patterns you'll become and the more likely it is that you won't fulfil your potential to be happy. You don't give yourself the chance to discover what you could actually be capable of, you don't learn how to manage challenges, and you don't give yourself the opportunity to feel good about yourself for having achieved something. So, you don't get to be happier.

It doesn't have to be this way!

Living according to your values, doing what's important to you and has meaning for you – being happy – does involve making an effort, persevering, taking some risks, and making sacrifices. It means stepping out of your comfort zone. But each time you extend your comfort zone you extend your happiness.

Happiness Habit: Look for Opportunities to Step Outside Your Comfort Zone

Write a list of five things you could do that would move you out of your comfort zone; things that won't involve too much of a stretch. Then choose one of the things on your list and do it.

Mel is an illustrator. 'Two years ago, I decided to leave my job as an illustrator to work freelance. I worried about changing from a secure income to an uncertain one but it had become important to me to have more flexible hours; more control over my days and pursue the type of illustrative work I was really interested in and liked doing.

The first year wasn't easy. Pitching for work, waiting to hear if I'd been successful and chasing invoices were the things I really didn't like about working freelance. I also had to get used to the change from working with five or six other people in a studio to just me on my own working in my flat.

Despite that, I'm happier! I've got the flexibility and control I was aiming for and I adapted to the changes and learnt to manage the challenges; I'm building up a list of clients who give me work and I've stopped spending so much time and energy getting het up about those clients that don't get back to me. I've dropped them. I'm also less stressed about unpaid invoices – they all pay up eventually. I've saved up an emergency fund so that I can cover my bills when clients don't pay on time.'

Is there something you'd like to do but, like all those people Bronnie Ware talked to, you can't or won't break out of your usual habits and routines? Think you can't adapt to change? Of course you can.

Happiness Habit: Practise Making Changes

You can prove to yourself that you can deal with change. Try, for example, driving, walking, or cycling a different route to somewhere you regularly go: to work, to the gym, to the pub, to visit friends or family. Take a different route from your normal one around the supermarket. Yes, it's an effort, but you can also see that doing things differently is not impossible.

Let Go of What's Making You Unhappy

Perhaps, though, you're not concerned about the challenges that might be involved in pursuing your goal or goals. That's not what's putting you off. Perhaps what's holding you back is that there's something you need to do or stop doing before you can commit and pursue what you'd like to do. What is it? What's getting in the way of pursuing your goals? Is there something you need to stop doing; something you need to let go of?

Maybe you need to leave a course, leave a relationship, drop a friendship, or move home. Maybe you're stuck in a job you really don't like. Or the job is OK but the commute is making you miserable. Perhaps you've committed yourself to something – a course, a cause, or some voluntary work – where even if you liked it at first, you're not enjoying it now. Perhaps the course is stressing you out and you're unhappy. Or your commitment to a cause or club is getting in the way of you doing things that are more important to you now. It's interfering with the life you want to live. Perhaps you're living somewhere that, for one or more reasons, is just not right for you. Or maybe you have a friendship that's draining you; you no longer have anything in common or, worse, one way or another your 'friend' has become toxic.

Why Can't You Let Go?

It could be that you tell yourself that you're used to, for example, the crappy job, the incompetent boss, and the sniping colleagues; you've put up with it all for so long that you might as well continue. Maybe you're thinking about all the time, effort, love, or money you've already put into something: the course, the friendship, the cause, or whatever. What would've been the point of all that if you cut loose now? Perhaps you're worried about letting people down if you pull out; they'll be disappointed or upset, offended or even angry if you tell them you no longer want to be involved in something that they rely on you for or that they think you 'should' be doing. Perhaps you don't want to call it a day because you don't want to admit that you made the wrong decision in the first place. Or you don't want to admit that you've continued with something that's been making you unhappy for so long.

Even though you're depressed and resentful, stressed or anxious, you push on, either believing there's nothing you can do or in the hope that things might somehow get better.

69

It's time to let go!

It's time to recognise that your priorities have changed. Instead of thinking that you 'ought' to stay or you might as well stick with something, think about what you'd really, really rather do. What's now more important to you, more in line with your values and priorities? What's more likely to make you happy? Be honest with yourself.

Positive and Negative Thinking

It could be that as a result of past experiences you have a tendency toward negative thinking; you've learnt to be helpless, hopeless, and resigned. You believe that you have no control over current and future situations and circumstances. You've told yourself there's no way out of problems and difficulties; there's nothing you can do to change things. In fact, you're unwilling to try.

Positive thinkers, on the other hand, see difficulties as not being permanent; they're a temporary setback.

This tendency to put the most favourable construction upon actions and events, or to anticipate the best possible outcome is, of course, optimism. Optimism allows you to feel in control of your life and believe there *is* something you can do to manage events. Optimism encourages you to look on the more positive side of events or conditions and to expect the most favourable outcome.

Happiness Habit: Think Positive!

Get into the habit of positive thinking. For any one thing you'd like to stop doing, to let go of, write down what you have to gain; how you would benefit. What would letting go then give you the time, freedom, space, or money to do?

Free Yourself from Commitments and Situations that Are Making You Unhappy

If you find it difficult to admit that you made a mistake, realise that at the time, you made the right choice. So yes, at the time it seemed like a good idea to, for example, enrol on the course, but now you realise it's not working out for you. Your feelings have changed.

This happened to Dev. A couple of years ago Dev got a place at university to study digital film production.

But at the end of the first term, he realised that it wasn't right for him. He realised that in three years' time, not only would he have a large debt, but even though he'd have a degree, he'd still have to start at the bottom of the film industry, as a runner. Dev knew he certainly didn't need a degree to be a runner. Rather than wait three years and have a £30000 debt, Dev wanted to start as a runner now. However, not only would he have to tell his parents and ask if he could move back home, but he'd also already incurred that term's student loan, his parents had paid for that term's student accommodation, and he'd have to negotiate a way out of the student accommodation contract that committed him to being there until the end of the first year. He also knew that he'd have to really push to get work as a runner in the film business. None of this was going to be easy.

That was a year ago. Dev dealt with all the difficulties involved in leaving his university course. He's taken every running job that's come up; he works long hours – 14-hour days are not unusual. He's progressed from working as a runner and has recently had two jobs as a trainee cameraman. He's happy.

Here's another example of someone realising that what they thought they wanted wasn't, after all, right for them; it wasn't making them happy.

At the same time as she received an inheritance sum from her mum, Lou was made redundant. She decided to leave her busy life, her grown-up sons and many friends in London, and move to a rural area in another part of the country. Rather than look for a job, Lou decided that she'd invest her inheritance and redundancy money in property – a couple of holiday cottages – and get an income from renting out the cottages. She enrolled on a property investment course.

After a year, Lou realised she'd made a mistake; she realised that property development and the holiday lettings business wasn't for her. And, although she now had a dog and she loved going out for long walks in the country with him, she was isolated, lonely, and bored.

Lou reappraised her values and her priorities. She realised just how important her friends, family, and her social life were to her. Lou also recognised that having colleagues and the structure and security of a regular job were important to her too.

Rather than thinking of herself as having made a mistake and failed, Lou saw herself as having an idea, pursuing it, and realising, quite simply, it wasn't making her happy. Yes, she would have lost some money, and she was apprehensive about telling her family and friends that she'd made a mistake. But rather than dwell on what she'd done 'wrong', Lou decided to call it a day. It took a lot of sorting out, but Lou did sort it out. She struggled to find somewhere affordable to live back in the south, and it took a while to get a job – in fact she has two part-time jobs – but she's a lot happier.

Are you in a situation where you're unhappy? Is there something else you'd rather be doing? What's stopping you from letting go? Perhaps you don't want to lose the time, energy, or money you've already invested. But, like Lou and Dev, you must focus on what you have to gain rather than what you have to lose by pulling out. Whether you've put up with it for a month, a year, or even half a lifetime, you shouldn't carry on letting yourself be miserable just because you think all that past misery would be wasted otherwise. Don't let the past dictate the present. Like Dev and Lou, know that what matters is how you live your life now.

Unless you signed a contract, there's nothing to stop you from walking away. In fact, even if you did sign a contract, you can work round that. (Dev had to negotiate a way out of his contract for student accommodation and he still has to pay back his first term's fees. In order to pursue his dream of working in film, he was prepared, quite literally, to pay the price.)

You may feel uncomfortable or even scared – you've got to explain your change of mind to friends, family, or colleagues – but having a few difficult conversations is a small price to pay for what's right for you from now on.

If your commitment was to one or more other people – if, for example, you no longer want to continue being involved with a club, a cause or campaign – give your reason, give as much notice as you can, and then leave. The other people will adjust; people can and will sort it out. They'll be fine. But if you stay in that situation, will you be fine? Or will you feel trapped and unhappy; stuck in a situation you don't like and unable to get on with what you now want to do?

You're not a bad person because you no longer want to be involved in something. Rather, you're a good person because you've recognised that something isn't right for you – your heart isn't in it and it's time to let go.

Free yourself from commitments and situations that you resent and that are making you unhappy.

Let go of relationships that are draining you. If a friendship has run its course, then let it fade. And if another person is making you seriously unhappy, if someone is bullying you – persistently badgering, dominating, or intimidating you, continually criticising, insulting, or humiliating you in person or online – you *must* do something. This person will not go away!

You can get help and support to deal with it (there's a list of websites for support and information at the back of this book). But you should also think about leaving; leaving the job, the neighbourhood, the relationship, or the social media account.

If you're being bullied, decide what's most important to you: surely it's the freedom to live your life in peace? Think about the good things that can happen if you choose to leave the situation. Yes, you might have to walk away from a good job, financial stability, friends, etc., but focus on the positive; that you've left the bully behind. By walking away, you put yourself in a positive position; one of being in control. You take away the opportunity for the bully to continue their behaviour. Once you have left them you can put your energy into finding a new job or somewhere to live instead of spending your energy trying to avoid, pacify, or please the bully.

The same principles apply to any situation that's making you unhappy and preventing you from getting on with your life; acknowledge what you have to lose by letting go but focus on what you have to gain. Then take the first step.

Take Steps

Whatever it is you need to do first; whatever it is you need to change, to stop doing or to let go of, that's the first step towards your goal. It's the first step towards what you really want to be doing. The process involved in dropping a commitment, letting go, or walking away from an unhappy situation, is pretty much the same process as described in Chapter 2.

1. *Identify the goal.* What, exactly, is it that you want to stop or drop?
2. *Identify the benefits.* What will you gain by letting go? How will you feel – relieved? Pleased? Overjoyed? What will letting go then free you up to do?
3. *Think through your options.* How might you pull out? What information, advice and support might you need? Think about who else could help; talk to others who have faced the same challenges; listen to how they coped. Also, think about how flexible you're prepared to be; whatever it is you want to stop doing, is your decision final? Or might you be prepared to negotiate and compromise? So if,

for example, you need to tell someone you can't run the charity, cause, or campaign anymore, are you going to pull out at the end of next month, or might you be prepared to stay until they've found someone to replace you?

4. *Identify the steps you'll take.* Whatever it is that you need to do, breaking it down into smaller, more doable steps can help make it far less daunting. It's probably not going to be easy, but once you've taken the first step you'll have got things started and you can deal with it from there. So, whether you need to ditch the job, leave the course, or let go of the friendship, take that first step. Write that letter. Send the email. Fill in the form. Make the appointment. Make that first phone call. Talk to the other person. Tell your friends and family. Get legal advice. Whatever it is that you need to do, take that first step and set the ball rolling!

Once you start doing something, it's easier to continue doing it. Take action and things will flow from there. That's why it helps to have a plan for the steps you need to take: it's easier if you know what you're doing first and what step comes next. Keep your mind focused on one step at a time. Tell yourself 'this is what I'm going to do next' and then just focus on that one step you're taking. Then take the next step, and you'll see yourself coping and moving forward.

You don't have to wait to feel confident and fearless before you get going. Get going and you'll just be getting on with it.

Have Courage!

Happy people aren't fearless, they're courageous. You can be the same; you can draw on your courage to take that first step and to manage the difficulties of letting go of a situation or relationship that's making you unhappy. Having courage doesn't mean *not* being afraid. Courage means doing something even though you *are* afraid and you know there are going to be difficulties and problems extricating yourself from a situation.

Whether it's standing up for yourself or someone else, making a decision that others won't like, leaving your job, course, or a relationship or moving home, courage is what makes you brave and helps you move forward in spite of your fears and concerns. Courage can also help you do what you want to do in spite of other people's fears or concerns, their objections or disapproval.

As the author and rock band manager James Hollingworth (aka Ambrose Redmoon) said: 'Courage is not the absence of fear but rather the determination that something else is more important.'

Isn't your happiness more important?

Happiness Habit: Be Courageous

Get into the habit of being courageous. Here's how.

Focus on the positive. Remind yourself *why* you want to do something; what you stand to gain. This can give you the motivation and courage you need to take the necessary first step. Focusing on why you're doing something and what you want to achieve – keeping that in your mind – can help stop feelings of doubt, uncertainty, and fear from taking over. So, focus on the benefits of letting go of something that's not making you happy. Think about being free to work towards, and achieving, what you'd really rather be doing.

Rather than fight feelings of fear and doubt, acknowledge and accept them. Tell yourself 'I'm feeling scared. I'm not sure about this'. Then push past those thoughts and feelings and tell yourself 'But I can do this'. Feel the fear. And then do it.

Don't overthink it. The more you think about whether you should or shouldn't do something, the longer you have to come up with excuses, and the less likely you are to take that first courageous step. Courage can be prone to leaking, so the longer you wait, the less of it you'll have. Once you've decided to do something, don't wait – do it!

Focus on the first step. Having thought through the steps, now just focus on that first step; on saying, for example, 'I have something to tell you'. So

(Continued)

(Continued)

often, taking the first step is half the battle, so pushing yourself over the threshold will create the momentum that will move things forward. And by then you'll just be dealing with it.

Get things in perspective. Understand that whatever it is you have to let go of and walk away from, as difficult to manage as it is, days and weeks or months and years from now it will be just something you had to deal with before you could change course and be free to do what makes you happy. Getting things into perspective helps you to recognise that whether you take action or not, life will continue. So, you might as well screw up your courage, take action, and make things work out so that as life continues, it does so in the ways you want it to.

Happiness Habit: Be Inspired

Inspire yourself. Think of a situation in the past when you felt afraid, yet faced your fear and took action. What helped? What was it that made you take that bold step?

Be inspired by other people. Talk to others about what changes they made in their lives; what they had to change, let go of, etc., in order to be happy. Ask them if they were anxious or scared; how did they deal with it? How did things turn out for them?

In a Nutshell

- Being happy – living according to your values, having goals, doing what is important to you and has meaning for you – involves making an effort, persevering, taking some risks, and making sacrifices. It means stepping out of your comfort zone. But each time you extend your comfort zone you extend your happiness.
- You can't change situations you don't take responsibility for. There will always be challenges and difficulties involved in pursuing happiness, but if you don't push yourself, nothing will change and you won't be happier.
- Maybe, though, there's something you need to stop doing; something you need to let go of before you can commit and pursue what you'd like to do.
- Maybe you're thinking about all the time, effort, love, or money you've already put into something. Maybe you've had particular routines and commitments for months or years. It's what you know, so you might as well carry on. Perhaps you're worried about letting people down if you pull out of a commitment, even though it's making you unhappy. Perhaps you don't want to admit that you made the wrong decision in the first place. Or you don't want to admit that you've continued with something that's been making you unhappy for so long.

(Continued)

(*Continued*)

- Even though you're depressed and resentful, stressed, or anxious, you push on, either believing there's nothing you can do to change things or just hoping that things might somehow get better.
- Instead of thinking that you 'ought' to stay or you 'might as well' stick with something, think about what you'd really, really rather do. What's now more important to you, more in line with your values and priorities? What's more likely to make you happy? Be honest with yourself.
- Free yourself from commitments and situations that are making you unhappy.
- If you find it difficult to admit that you made a mistake, realise that, at the time, you made the right choice, but now you realise it's not working out for you. Your feelings have changed.
- Explaining your change of mind to friends, family, or colleagues is a small price to pay for what's right for you from now on. The other people will adjust; people can and will sort it out. But if you stay in that situation you'll feel trapped and unhappy; stuck in a situation you don't like and unable to get on with what you now want to do.
- Let go of relationships that are draining you. And if another person is making you seriously unhappy, you must do something about it.
- For any situation that's making you unhappy and preventing you from getting on with your life, acknowledge what you have to lose by letting go but focus on what you have to gain. Then take the first step.

- The process involved in dropping a commitment, letting go, or walking away from an unhappy situation is the same process involved in creating meaning and purpose in your life: identify your goal, identify the benefits – what will you gain by letting go? Think through your options: how might you pull out? What information, advice, and support might you need? Identify the steps you'll take; whatever it is that you need to do, breaking it down into smaller, more doable steps can help make it far less daunting.

- Draw on your courage to take that first step and to manage the difficulties of letting go of a situation or relationship that's making you unhappy. Having courage doesn't mean not being afraid. Courage means doing something even though you're afraid and you know there's going to be difficulties and problems extricating yourself.

Happiness Habits

- Look for opportunities to step outside your comfort zone.
- Practise making changes; see that doing things differently is not impossible.
- Think positive! For any one thing you'd like to stop doing, to let go of, write down what you have to gain; how you would benefit.

(Continued)

(*Continued*)

- Be courageous. Acknowledge then push past feelings of fear and doubt and tell yourself 'but I can do this'. Focus on the first step. Don't overthink it. Feel the fear. And then do it.
- Be inspired. Think of past situations when you felt afraid, yet faced your fear and took action. Ask other people if, when they wanted to let go of something, they were anxious or scared and how did they deal with it?
- Get things into perspective. Days and weeks or months and years from now, it will be just something you had to deal with before you could change course and be free to do what makes you happy.
- Focus on the benefits of letting go of something that's not making you happy. Think about being free to work towards and achieve what you'd really rather be doing.

4

How to Be Happy: Identify and Indulge in Small Pleasures

Leisure

What is this life if, full of care,
We have no time to stand and stare.
No time to stand beneath the boughs
And stare as long as sheep or cows.

– W.H. Davies

The first four lines of W.H. Davies's poem remind us that, too often, we're so caught up in cares and worries and rushing from one thing to the next that we have no time to stand and stare; we miss the small pleasures.

Small Pleasures and Awesome Things

Whatever your circumstances, whatever your abilities, there's a world of small pleasures which can bring you moments of happiness every day. We all have things that we enjoy, that give us pleasure and moments of happiness.

What, for you, makes for a small pleasure? A bubble bath, a hot shower, warm towels? Fresh, clean sheets? A book by one of your favourite authors, listening to a favourite piece of music or watching a great film? Maybe, on a cold morning, it's putting on an item of clothing that's been sitting on a hot radiator. Maybe eating the froth on the cappuccino is one of your small pleasures. What about a lie in? A kiss, a cuddle, or holding hands? Perhaps it's an open fire, sitting in the sun, or a walk in the rain. Maybe talking to your dog or cat is one of your small pleasures.

Life is a collection of moments and the more happy moments we have, the more often we are happy.

Canadian author Neil Pasricha has managed to identify 1000 small pleasures. He's listed them on his website 1000AwesomeThings.com. Here are a few that might resonate with you:

Singing the national anthem with a big crowd
Successfully navigating your way home in the dark
Looking through the little window in the oven
Seeing a dog or cat chasing its own tail
Waiters and waitresses who know the menu really well
The first warm day of spring
Dogs with jobs

The sound of a golf ball falling into the cup
Car dancing
When a deadline is extended unexpectedly
The smell of really, really clean air
Putting things in your shoe so you don't forget them later
Eating a free sample of something you have no intention of buying
When the bass kicks in
Putting a slice of lasagne on a plate and having it stay all together
Having a staring contest with a baby
When the mug you're warming up in the microwave stops with the handle pointing towards you
When everyone you're eating with at the restaurant agrees you made the best choice
That bite with all the toppings in it
When someone calls just to say hi
When you hit that point in the book where you suddenly can't stop reading
When babies grab at your face with their tiny hands
Throwing non-ball objects to people
Drying off in the sun after swimming
When you continue talking through the yawn and your friend actually understands you
Flying over mountains
People who look like their pets
Watching the Christmas episode of your favourite sitcom in the completely wrong month

Just reading a few of Neil Pasricha's 'awesome things' each day is, in itself, a small pleasure!

Happiness Habit: Make a List of the Things that Make You Happy

Be mindful; make the effort to notice what's happening around you that pleases you. When you make an effort to notice things, you'll be surprised at just how many things make you smile and lift your spirits.

Get into the habit of identifying and indulging in small pleasures; the ordinary and the extraordinary, the familiar and the new, the small things and the bigger things. The cheap and the expensive, the easily accessible and the things that are hard to find or to come by.

Look out for what makes you smile and surround yourself with it as much as you can.

– Ilona Burton

Happiness Habit: Start Your Day with a Smile

I have a friend – Keith – who starts the day by watching an episode of the American sitcom 'Frasier' every morning. He says it gets his day off to a good start. You could do the same; start your day with an episode of a favourite sitcom or podcast.

Can Money Buy Happiness?

Some small pleasures are free, some are cheap, and some are expensive. The big question is, can money buy you happiness? We've all been told that money can't buy happiness but many studies have shown that's not really true; money *can* buy you happiness.

You don't, though, need a fortune before money can buy you happiness. What's important is knowing *what* to spend your money on; knowing how to spend it in ways that are more likely to make you happy.

In 2011, in *The Journal of Consumer Psychology*, Professor Elizabeth Dunn and her colleagues published a paper based on their review of research into how money does and doesn't make us happy. The title of the paper? *If money doesn't make you happy then you probably aren't spending it right.*

They suggest that 'Money is an opportunity (for happiness) that people routinely squander because the things they think will make them happy often don't'. Professor Dunn and her colleagues' key finding was that rather than spend money on things in the hope they'll make us happy, we should spend it on experiences.

Buy Experiences Instead of Things
In their report, Professor Dunn and her colleagues explain that the *type* of experiences – the activities you

spend your money on – aren't that important; it could be something simple and inexpensive such as doing a jigsaw or taking a bus ride to the country or the coast, or it could be something more costly – a flying lesson or a day at a spa. As far as happiness is concerned, what's most important about any activity you engage in is that you *are* engaged in the activity; you're interested and absorbed in the experience.

In other words, you experience 'Flow'. You will have experienced Flow whenever you've become so absorbed in what you're doing that time passed without you noticing. You were doing something that was enjoyable and kept you focused and engaged. It was as if a water current was carrying you along, continuously and smoothly.

Just as with Aristotle's eudaimonic happiness, when you're involved in an activity that gives you a sense of Flow, you're doing something that's meaningful; there's a purpose and an aim to what you're doing. Even though there may be an element of challenge to the activity, it's enjoyable, there's progression, and it maintains your interest. You feel fulfilled. You're happy.

Happiness Habit: Make Flow Happen in Your Life

Think about what you already do that gives you a sense of Flow; maybe it's your job or particular aspects of your work; it could be the interests, hobbies, and things you do in your spare time. Do more of what you enjoy and do what you enjoy more often.

Free and Inexpensive Activities

If you need some ideas, there are plenty of activities you can do that will give you a sense of Flow. Here are some that cost very little or are free.

Drawing. All you need is some paper and a pencil. But what if you've got no artistic talent? Illustrator and portrait painter Gilly Lovegrove (www. gillylovegroveillustration.com) believes everyone has. She says that 'with the right tuition/guidance, a positive attitude and allowing time to the subject, anyone can learn to draw'.

Photography. There's no need to buy an expensive camera; assuming you've already got a phone with a camera, brilliant results can be obtained with a camera phone.

For both drawing and photography you'll find instructional videos on YouTube: www.youtube. co.uk.

Origami. To get started, just get yourself a pack of origami paper. Everything you need to know can be found on the British Origami Society website. Details of clubs near to you can also be found on their website: http://www.britishorigami.info/society/meetings/. Instructional videos can also be found on YouTube.

Learn a language. You can sign up to a class but you can also learn on your own, for free. Go to Duolingo: www.duolingo.com. As the Duolingo strapline says: 'Learn a language for free. Forever'.

Writing. If you can read, you can write. Try poems or short stories. Try writing stories for children. Keep a journal, write your life story, start a blog.

Cooking. You've got to eat. You're going to spend money on food anyway. You could use it as an opportunity to learn new recipes. Go to www.bbc.co.uk/food for a wide range of recipes.

Bird-watching. The RSPB says 'You don't need much to enjoy birds – just your eyes or ears. But there are lots of things which can make it easier or more enjoyable. We have advice on buying the right kit to help you get off to a great start': www.rspb.org.uk.

Spotting a Red-breasted Boubou for the first time or tracing the flight of a Sparrowhawk across the hills represent different kinds of excitement to watching England take on Wales in rugby. But they're thrills all the same ... A love of ornithology is something I'll carry with me for the rest of my life.

– BBC broadcaster Matthew Stadlen

Juggling and magic tricks. Get three scarves or balls. Failing that, ball up some socks. Learn some magic tricks. Watch a few YouTube instructional videos and practise until you're perfect!

Try out some activities with no expectation other than to see what they're like. Here are some more ideas for activities that can give you a sense of Flow and moments of pleasure:

Team sports such as football, rugby, netball, hockey, basketball, volleyball. Activities such as swimming, judo, tennis, horse riding, rock climbing, and rowing. If you enjoy them, they'll keep you completely engaged.

Singing and dancing. Join a choir or dance class or simply sing and dance along to your favourite tunes in the kitchen.

Creative interests. Gardening, DIY, painting, sewing, writing music, playing a musical instrument. Whatever it is, a creative activity can totally engage you.

Games and puzzles. Whether it's card and board games, computer games, jigsaws, crosswords, or sudoku, all require a level of concentration and provide a challenge that will have you totally absorbed.

Books and films. It could be a gripping thriller, science fiction, or a clever comedy. Whatever the genre, as events unfold, you become lost in the story.

Make time for personal interests such as a hobby or physical activity. As often as possible, do something that gives you moments of pleasure and makes you happy. It's easy to let personal time slip away, especially when we're stressed or overloaded with work. However much or little money you have, do whatever it takes to find the time for activities that you enjoy and that engage you.

Happiness Habit: Plan for Things to Look Forward to

Whether it's a day or a night out with friends, a weekend away, a holiday, or an adventure, get something booked and put into your diary or calendar. Even if it's weeks or months from now. Then, whenever you need a shot of happiness, remind yourself about it.

Happiness Habit: Do Things that Relate to Your Values; Things that Are Important to You

Taking part or just watching sports, for example, provides opportunities to experience values such as belonging, loyalty, teamwork, cooperation, support, discipline, competing, winning, succeeding, excitement, and enjoyment. Cultural activities – the arts, film, theatre, music – whether it's taking part, viewing, watching, or listening – can reflect values such as beauty and harmony, enjoyment, creativity, curiosity, and learning.

Experiences Can Last Longer than Things

When it comes to spending money in order to be happy, you might think that it's better to spend it on things rather than activities and experiences because things last longer. Surely, you might think, the money spent on, for example, a great new pair of shoes is money better spent towards your happiness than money spent on an experience such as a day out? An experience, you could argue, is over after a few hours or days, whereas a lovely new pair of shoes can last you a lot longer.

But after the initial thrill of buying something – lovely new shoes, a super new computer, a smartphone, a fab new sofa – the excitement soon wears off. This is because you get used to it. The great new shoes become just another pair of shoes that you own. The computer and smartphone become things you need for work and your daily life. And the fab new sofa soon just becomes the place where you sit and watch TV; quite literally, it becomes part of the furniture – something so familiar that you no longer notice it. Of course, a sofa, phone, computer, and lovely shoes are all useful, but after a while, you don't think of those things in the same excited way as you did when you first owned them.

In contrast, an experience can provide you with happy memories long after the shoes and sofa have worn out and the phone and computer have stopped working.

Certainly, both experiences and things provide the positive feelings that come with looking forward to them. But once they're over, you're more likely to relive experiences – a picnic with friends, hot air ballooning, learning to cook Japanese food, a day at the beach, tea at The Ritz, tank driving – than you are likely to recall the things you bought in the past. And even the disappointing and the disastrous days out usually make for a funny story in the retelling, whereas a disappointing or disastrous purchase always remains just that; a disappointing purchase.

What to Buy and What Not to Buy

But if experiences have the potential to make you happier than things, does that mean that it's pointless spending money – particularly spending a lot of money – on things; that things won't make you happy? No, buying things *can* make you happy. It's knowing *what* things to buy that will most likely make you happy. And it's knowing what things *not* to buy.

To start with, buy things that help you to have pleasurable experiences. If you have a hobby or interest – playing sport or creating art, for example – that you enjoy and that makes you happy, spend your money on the things that support that hobby or interest: sports equipment, art materials, and so on.

You should also spend your money on things that will make your life easier. If, for example, you work from home and spend a lot of time sitting at a desk, even though it's not a particularly exciting purchase, buy the best chair that you can afford. If buying a bike enables you to get to work more easily, then spend your money on a bike. On the other hand, if you rarely go for a bike ride, a bicycle you hardly ever use could just feel like a pricey item in the shed. And that won't make you happy!

Think about what's important to you. You spend a third of your life in bed; a good night's sleep is important to set you up for managing the ups and downs of the next day. So maybe you could buy the best mattress you can. If your bedroom is cold in winter, you might want to spend your money on an electric blanket. Last winter, my friends Bill and Ali bought an electric blanket. They told me 'Every single night we say how happy we are to have bought it'. And if, for example, you find that listening to music or podcasts helps you get to sleep, but trying to sleep with earbuds hurts your ears and gets you tangled up in wires, buying a speaker that goes under your pillow will be money well spent.

Before we value anything, the fact that we value anything at all is because we have first seen it and registered its value.

– Alex Ratcliffe

And if you do a lot of ironing, a handheld steamer to de-wrinkle your clothes might not fill you with joy, but it could make your life easier. If you have a disability, then mobility aids and daily living products can improve your independence and make everyday life that little bit easier – and happier.

Spend money on services that allow you to avoid doing what you don't like doing or struggle to do; a cleaner for your home, for example, a decorator or the services of a gardener. Spend money on experiences you enjoy – pay others to do the things you don't enjoy doing.

> ### Happiness Habit: Support Businesses that Share Your Values
>
> If, for example, community is important to you, consider spending more of your money at local shops and independent retailers.

> ### Happiness Habit: Appreciate the Things You Already Own
>
> Earlier in this chapter, you will have read that after the initial thrill of buying something – lovely new shoes, a super new computer, a smartphone, a fab new sofa – the excitement wears off. This is because you get used to it. You no longer get a thrill from using or wearing it. It doesn't have to be this way. Appreciate the things you already own. Make a point of noticing and acknowledging the benefits and pleasures your things have brought you, so that your pleasure in them doesn't wear off.

What Not to Buy

A friend who once owned a boat told me: 'There's an old joke that says the happiest two days of a boat owner's life are the day they buy their boat – and the day they sell it.' We all know that boats are expensive to buy. But they're also expensive to keep. 'Before you buy anything that has an engine and floats on water,' my friend told me, 'you need to think about the costs of financing, insuring, and maintaining it. There's also transportation costs, fuel, mooring fees, cleaning fees, and winter storage fees. And all for something you might only use for a few months each year.'

There aren't many of us who can afford to buy a boat, but the principle holds true; when it comes to something you're thinking of buying, be aware of the commitments that might come with it that could turn the dream purchase into an obligation and a burden. Too often, when we imagine how happy we'd be to own something – a boat, a car, a second home – we tend to forget the extra costs and the hassle we'll incur. It happens to wealthy celebrities too. George Clooney bought a Tesla Roadster as a toy – and had to sell the thing because, he said, he was 'always stuck on the side of the f—— road with it'.

Happiness Habit: Hire Happiness

Learn to enjoy things without owning them. Ownership is nothing, access is everything.

– Joshua Becker

Instead of splashing out on buying an expensive boat, another option is to rent a boat several times each year instead. You'll spend a lot less money without all the extra costs and hassle, but still have all the fun and enjoyment. And you could do the same with a car. If it's an expensive open-top sports car you're after, hire a fancy sports car for a weekend away. Extravagant? Yes. But it's a lot less than buying a new car and gives you

(Continued)

(*Continued*)

a memorable experience which won't wear off because, not only do you not have the associated costs and hassle, you don't become used to it, so each time you hire it you get a burst of happiness!

It's not just expensive luxury goods that you can hire or rent. Support your local library. Borrow adult and children's fiction and non-fiction books and eBooks. Audio books, language courses, music scores, and books in other languages are also available to borrow.

And it's not just books that you can borrow – how about borrowing someone else's dog? If you'd love a dog but can't commit 24/7, have look at www.borrowmydoggy. com. It connects dog owners with local dog lovers to share the care of a dog.

Buy Many Small Pleasures Instead of a Few Big Ones

In their report, 'If money doesn't make you happy then you probably aren't spending it right', Professor Dunn and her colleagues suggest that because the initial thrill of buying something soon wears off, when we do buy things, 'It may be better to indulge in a variety of frequent, small pleasures'.

However, the problem with this advice is that it appears to give us permission to buy lots of cheap things. But in this day and age, we all need to accumulate less stuff. So, what to do? You don't need to stop buying things completely, but you can make conscious and deliberate decisions about what you buy.

Happiness Habit: Buy Good Quality Things that You Need, Not Lots of Random Stuff that Appeals Just Because it's so Cheap

An occasional purchase is a pleasure to indulge (I like expensive hand cream; it's a small pleasure every time I use it), but for many of us, we need to rein in the constant buying and accumulating. What to do? Anytime you feel yourself tempted to buy more cheap stuff – something you don't really need – surf the urge. Imagine the urge to buy as a wave in the ocean. It will build in intensity, but soon break and dissolve. Imagine yourself riding the wave, not fighting it but also not giving in to it. Know that cravings aren't permanent, they come and then they go. Just like the waves.

Spend Money on Other People

Things, then, *can* make us happy. The things we buy are more likely to contribute to our happiness if they support our interests and make our daily lives easier. And if we make a point of appreciating them.

In their review of research into how money does and doesn't make us happy, Professor Elizabeth Dunn and her colleagues found that as well as spending our money on experiences, the research suggests spending our money on others can greatly contribute towards our happiness.

In their review, Professor Dunn and her colleagues write that 'Given how deeply and profoundly social we are, it isn't any wonder that the quality of our social relationships is a strong determinant of our happiness. Because of this, almost anything we do to improve our connections with others tends to improve our happiness as well – and that includes spending money.'

Spending money on other people doesn't mean just giving them cash or buying them random things – trinkets and baubles, ornaments and gadgets. Those sorts of things are nice gifts, but the research shows that we'll get the most happiness from buying things that will help others – that will make a positive difference to their lives.

Equipment to make their lives easier, for example, or to facilitate an interest or hobby they have: lessons, books for their studies, vouchers to learn a new skill; anything from flying lessons and land yachting to art, music, or dance lessons, a bus or train pass, car valeting, or the services of a cleaner or gardener.

Positive Relationships

Understand that friends come and go, but for the precious few you should hold on. Work hard to bridge the gaps in geography and lifestyle, because the older you get, the more you need the people you knew when you were young.

– Mary Schmich

Another reason why experiences have the potential to make us happier than things is that experiences are likely to be shared with other people, and time with other people – with friends and other people we like and whose company we enjoy – can be a source of happiness. In his book *Flourish*, positive psychology professor Martin Seligman suggests that as well as needing meaning, purpose, and short-lived pleasures in our lives, to be happy we need to interact with others; to connect and feel that we belong. In other words, we need positive relationships.

Who are the positive people in your life? Who do you enjoy spending time with? Who makes you laugh; is fun and lively to be with? With whom do you have shared interests? Who in your life is supportive and encouraging?

The positive people in your life do not just have to be friends or family; they could be colleagues or neighbours. The person you could talk to if you were worried or you could call on in a crisis could be your GP, a support worker, or a therapist. The people who appreciate you could be people you help through some voluntary work that you do.

For every positive person out there, however, there is often a negative person. Other people can sometimes be seen as 'radiators' or 'drains': radiators spread warmth and positivity, while drains take away your energy and resources; they're likely to sap your energy and discourage you.

It is not always possible or practical to remove negative people from your life. What you can do, however, is reduce the amount of time you spend around drains and increase the amount of time you spend with radiators, the positive people on your list.

That's not to suggest you distance yourself from anyone who's going through a difficult period in their life and needs your help and support (more on this in Chapter 6); in fact, if you are trying to cope with someone else, you *definitely* need radiators in your life to support you as you support someone else who is struggling.

Just being around radiators – their positivity is catching – makes you feel good. Research shows that positivity is contagious. In 2008, Professors James Fowler from the University of California, San Diego and Nicholas Christakis from Harvard University published findings from research that observed the spread of happiness over 20 years in one community. There were happy and unhappy groups of people in the network. People who were surrounded by happy people were more likely to become happy in the future. It appears that this wasn't just because happy people tended to inter-act with other happy people, but because people were more likely to become happy when they were around happy people.

You can test for yourself the idea that happiness is con-tagious; have a look at the YouTube videos 'Man Gobbles at Turkeys Turkeys Gobble Back', 'Laughing Man' and

'Contagious Subway Laughter'. See how quickly you start laughing too.

Happiness Habit: Spend Time with Positive People

As far as possible, reduce the amount of time you spend with negative people who drain you and increase the amount of time you spend with the positive people in your life; do what you can to spend time and do things with friends and family whose company you enjoy.

Anything you do to improve your connections with others will likely improve your happiness as well. Reach out to others; show interest, care, and concern to your friends, family, and colleagues. Invite others to join you in an activity or experience. Know that just as creating meaning and purpose in your life takes time and effort, connecting with other people – having good relationships with others – also takes time and effort.

Happiness Habit: Meet People and Make New Friends

If you need more positive relationships in your life, start to meet new people. Meet people who share the same interests. Of course, making new friends isn't always easy. It takes effort on your part; you need to be willing to meet others, to be yourself and give something of yourself. You

(Continued)

(*Continued*)

can make new friends, but you can't sit and wait for other people to come to you. You need to get out there!

Have a look at www.meetup.com. meetup.com enables people to find and join groups of other people in their local area who share each other's interests. There are groups to fit a wide range of interests and hobbies, plus others you'll never have thought of. There are book groups, art groups, film groups, sci-fi groups, gardening groups, singing groups, and cycling groups.

People who go to 'Meetups' do so knowing they'll be meeting others who are also open to making new friends. If you find people who are just as keen on, for example, board games, Nordic walking, or craft beers as you are, then you'll find it relatively easy to connect and make friends with them. And when you're doing something that's fun and meaningful, your ability to form connections will come naturally.

Volunteer

Another way to connect with other people and experience positive relationships is through volunteering for a cause or local community initiative that interests you. Doing something to benefit someone else can make you and the person you are helping feel good. Studies show that helping others creates feelings and attitudes that can lead to better physical health, better mental health, and overall happiness.

Volunteers can do almost anything: support adults to learn to read, mentor ex-offenders, be involved in a conservation and environmental cause or visit people who are socially isolated. Whatever you do as a volunteer, you can make a vital contribution to any number of aspects of community life.

Volunteering is also a good way to meet people – other volunteers – and make friends. You can meet and create bonds with people who want to make a contribution to the lives of others; you have a common cause that is another opportunity to create meaning and purpose in your life.

Happiness Habit: Appreciate Three Things

I think if we took more time to stop and think how lucky we are and focus on these things we often forget to appreciate, we'd be happier. You and I should try that.

– Ilona Burton

At the end of each day – write down three good things that have happened that day. Just make an effort for a couple of weeks to identify the good things – the small pleasures – in your day. After a while, identifying and reflecting on the small pleasures will become a habit. A happiness habit.

Perhaps you had a good hair day. Your favourite song came on the radio at the perfect moment. Or you ate a

(Continued)

(*Continued*)

perfectly ripe avocado. Perhaps today was, for you, the perfect temperature (a study in Japan found that happiness is maximised at around 13.9 °C). Maybe something arrived that you forgot you'd ordered online. Or you managed to fix something: a cupboard door or a knot in a necklace. Maybe you dropped your phone, thought the screen had smashed but then realised it hadn't. Or it could be that you arrived late to meet someone only to find the other person was even later. Perhaps you received a humorous text from a friend or your dog did something that made you laugh.

I never fail to enjoy the sight of a female vicar smoking a fag. I've got no idea why this is, but I spotted one at Westfield a few months ago and it made my entire day.

– Ben Machell

Even if you have a bad day, find three good things that happened. You could write them down in a notebook, or you might simply reflect on what those things were while you're brushing your teeth. Appreciate just knowing that you had good in your day so that, whatever else happened, you know that you did have things that made it all worthwhile. Do this before you go to bed every night, and no matter what happened that day, you go to bed happy.

So yes, you missed the train, but, for example, it was a really good cup of coffee that you drank while waiting for the next train, or you met someone you hadn't seen for ages or you didn't have to stand in the rain; the waiting room was nice and warm. No, you didn't get offered the job, but at least they took the trouble to phone and give you feedback which was helpful. And, thankfully, you had an umbrella in your bag and avoided getting soaked in that downpour on your way home this evening.

Enjoy the little things, for one day you may look back and realise they were the big things.

– Robert Brault

In a Nutshell

- Whatever your circumstances, whatever your abilities, there's a world of small pleasures which can bring you moments of happiness every day. The more happy moments you have, the more often you can be happy.
- Whether you have a little or a lot of money, what's most important is knowing *what* to spend your money on; knowing how to spend it in ways that are more likely to make you happy.
- Rather than spend money on things in the hope they'll make you happy, spend it on activities and experiences.
- What's most important about any experience or activity you engage in is that you *are* engaged; you're interested and absorbed in the experience; you're involved in a way that gives you a sense of 'Flow'.

(Continued)

(*Continued*)

- When it comes to spending money in order to be happy, you might think that it's better to spend it on things rather than activities and experiences because things last longer. But after the initial thrill of buying something, after a while, you don't think of those things in the same excited way as you did when you first owned them. This is because you get used to them.
- Both experiences and things provide the positive feelings that come with looking forward to them. But once they're over, you're more likely to relive experiences. Experiences can provide you with happy memories long after the things you buy – the shoes and sofa, the phone or the computer – have worn out or stopped working.
- Even the disappointing and the disastrous days out usually make for a funny story in the retelling, whereas a disappointing or disastrous purchase remains just that; a disappointing purchase.
- However, even though experiences have the potential to make you happier than things, buying things *can* make you happy. It's knowing *what* things to buy that will most likely make you happy. And it's knowing what things *not* to buy.
- Buy things that help you to have pleasurable experiences. If you have a hobby or interest – playing sport or creating art, for example – that you enjoy and makes you happy, spend your money on the things that support that hobby or interest: sports equipment, art materials, and so on.
- Spend your money on things that will make your life easier. Spend money on services that allow you

to avoid doing what you don't like doing or struggle to do; spend time and money on experiences you enjoy – pay others to do the things you don't enjoy.

- Make conscious and deliberate decisions about what you buy. Make a point of appreciating the things you've bought; regularly remind yourself of why you like your things, be more aware of the ways they're useful or enjoyable.

- Be aware of the commitments that might turn the dream purchase into an obligation and a burden. Too often, when we imagine how happy we'd be to own something, we tend to forget the extra costs and the hassle we'll incur.

- Almost anything we do to improve our connections with others tends to improve our happiness as well. The research suggests spending our money on others can greatly contribute towards our happiness.

- Spend money in ways that will help others – that will make a positive difference to their lives. Equipment or services to make their lives easier, for example, or to facilitate an interest or hobby they have.

- Another reason why experiences have the potential to make us happier than things is that experiences are likely to be shared with other people, and time with other people – with friends and other people we like and whose company we enjoy – can be a source of happiness.

- Reach out to others; make time and make the effort to show interest, care, and concern to your friends, family, and colleagues. Invite others to join you in an activity or experience.

(*Continued*)

(*Continued*)

- Connect with other people by volunteering for a cause or local community initiative that interests you. Volunteering is an opportunity to create meaning and purpose in your life. Doing something to benefit someone else can make you and the person you are helping feel good. It's also a good way to meet people – other volunteers – and make friends.

Happiness Habits

- Make a list of the things that please you; identify and indulge in small pleasures.
- Start your day with a smile; start your day with an episode of a favourite sitcom or podcast.
- Make 'Flow' happen in your life. Do more of what you enjoy and do what you enjoy more often.
- Plan for things to look forward to. Even if it's for weeks or months from now.
- Do things that relate to your values; things that are important to you. Support businesses that share your values.
- Buy good quality things that you need, not lots of random stuff that appeals just because it's so cheap.
- Appreciate the things you already own. Make a point of noticing and acknowledging the benefits and pleasures your things have brought you, so that your pleasure in them doesn't wear off.

- Hire happiness. When it's possible and appropriate, hire and borrow things rather than buying them. You'll spend a lot less money without all the extra costs and hassle, but with all the fun and enjoyment.
- Reduce the amount of time you spend around negative people (drains) and increase the amount of time you spend with positive people (radiators).
- If you need more positive relationships in your life, start to meet new people.
- At the end of each day, write down three good things that have happened that day. Even if you have a bad day, find three good things that happened.

5
Happiness When Life Is Really Hard

But there are times when happiness really does seem impossible, incomprehensible even. It could be a few weeks of darkness during times of stress or after some upset, but sometimes it continues and grows and the thought of being happy becomes a foreign concept.

– Ilona Burton

To be happy – to find meaning and purpose, to identify small pleasures, to connect with others – certainly takes some thought and effort, but the real challenge to being happy comes when you're stuck in a situation that is making you unhappy and you can see no way out. When you find yourself in one of these situations, heed the advice in this chapter.

Being Stuck in a Job You Don't Like

Many people work in jobs that make them unhappy. It could be, for example, that your work is meaningless and dull. Perhaps you're bored and unchallenged, or your job is stressful; you feel overworked and unappreciated, or you hate your boss and don't like your colleagues, clients, or customers. Much as you'd love to, for whatever reason, right now, you can't quit. So, what can you do?

Think Positive

First, know that no matter how bad things are, you can always make things worse. Beware of confirmation bias. Confirmation bias happens when you look for evidence to support and confirm what you've already decided is true: that your job is crap. With confirmation bias it's easy to give too much weight to negative aspects and too little to the positive elements of a situation. If, for example, your boss fails to take control of a meeting – it drags on and nothing gets finalised – you not only think back and remember other times he's shown incompetence, you actually look out for other things that are 'wrong'; you look for evidence that just goes to confirm his incompetence.

The more you dislike your job or aspects of your job, the more you'll find evidence to back up your dislike. 'See? They're making me do all the name tags for the event. It's ridiculous. There are more important things I could be doing.' Your life becomes a day-to-day exercise in proving yourself right.

Whatever the problem is, by focusing so intently on it you're choosing to make yourself unhappy.

Be aware that when negativity controls your thoughts, it limits your behaviour, actions, and opportunities. Stop with the negativity and instead, if you can't leave, look for the positive aspects of your job. Is your job close to home and so you have a short journey to work? Is your commute a long one but you get to listen to the radio in the car or you get to read, listen to, or watch something on a tablet on the train? Your boss might be awful but maybe your colleagues are great.

If you are truly stuck there, you have to find a way to make the best of it. The way to do that is not only to focus on the positive, but also to focus on what you *can* control. Instead of making yourself miserable railing against the things you can't change, look to see what you *can* change.

As Reinhold Niebuhr's 'Serenity Prayer' says: 'God grant me the serenity to accept the things I cannot change; courage to change the things I can; and wisdom to know the difference.'

Negotiate Your Hours
Perhaps you have the sort of job where you could negotiate a day working from home. Or maybe you could reduce your hours. If you think you could manage on less money, asking to reduce your hours can be an effective way to spend less time working somewhere that

you're unhappy and give you more time and space to pursue interests outside of your job. You'll feel less defined by the job; it won't be such a dominant part of your life. Working fewer hours could also free you up to look for other jobs and attend interviews.

Make Your Job Work for You; Create Your Own Meaning and Purpose

Whether or not you can work from home or reduce your hours, if you're currently stuck in a job you don't like, aim to take charge of your own professional and personal development.

Set yourself a challenge. Choose an aspect of your job that is particularly onerous, difficult, boring, irritating, etc. Then set yourself a challenge to make it less difficult, boring, or irritating. Maybe you have a job where you often have to listen to other people's complaints. Take it on as a challenge; make it your goal to become really good at managing and resolving customer complaints.

Is there something missing – something that relates to your values – that you could bring into your work? Perhaps, for example, you'd like your work to have more social impact.

Here's what Sean did: 'I got in touch with local charities and community groups to discuss ways that our company could collaborate with them to provide services to help a client group that was completely different from our main client group. Not only did I start enjoying my job more, it also gave me the kind of experience I wanted for the work I knew that I really wanted to do in future.'

Maybe you could take the lead on initiating changes and improvements at work: a more comfortable working environment, or more efficient methods and procedures, or a flexible working policy. If you're feeling unfulfilled and unhappy, finding the motivation to take the lead on something probably isn't going to feel like the obvious and enjoyable thing to do. But it does provide you with some meaning and purpose in your working week and it will give you an extra skill for your next job.

In fact, just because you're not able to leave your job right now doesn't mean you can't start working towards the next one. What would you like to do in your next job – is there a skill you'll need that you can develop in your current job?

Think about developing a skill or an aspect of your job that you're already quite good at or enjoy doing. Maybe the one part of your job you enjoy is presenting pitches to potential clients. So, develop your presentation skills. Take a free online course. Watch a few TED talks – www.ted.com – pick out the best presenters, decide what's good about their presentation skills, and aim to do the same. Practise. Whatever aspect of your job you like, do whatever you need to do to get really, really good at it and make it as large a part of your job as you can.

You have to decide for yourself that you're going to make it personally meaningful. But if you can't develop new skills and challenges related to your work, then look for other ways you can learn new skills.

Alex, for example, was saving to travel in South America for six months. He had a night job stacking shelves at a supermarket. The work was extremely boring, dull, and repetitive. But he downloaded a language course so that while he was stacking shelves, he learnt Spanish.

You can learn new skills – re-train, study – in your lunchtime, on your commute, in the evenings or at weekends. Izzy, for example, decided to learn how to code. 'I knew it would be a useful skill, something that I could do freelance in future and it would enable me to work on my own terms. I signed up to two courses: one online and one in person at a local adult learning centre. I've enjoyed learning how to code. Now, in all the boring meetings at work, instead of getting wound up thinking what a waste of time it all is, I'm planning my next website or solving a programming problem in my head. Having something different and enjoyable to focus on has helped me to be happier.'

Happiness Habit: Make Time in Your Working Day for Small Pleasures

Have something to look forward to each lunchtime.

One day a couple of years ago, Laura Archer started to draw up a list of things she could do in her lunch break.

She thought she'd struggle to come up with more than a dozen ideas but after a few days, she was surprised to see that she'd come up with a list of 40 things. Was it, she wondered, possible to come up with 52 ideas – a different idea for each week of the year? Turns out it was. You can discover for yourself all of Laura's ideas in her book *Gone For Lunch. 52 things to do in your lunch break*.

Serious Difficulties, Setbacks, and Trauma

So, although it requires a lot of thought and effort, there *are* things you can do to make the best out of a bad job. How, though, can you find any happiness when you've suffered or are currently suffering a serious difficulty? Perhaps you recently lost something or someone you love; you've experienced a bereavement or a relationship break-up. Perhaps you've lost your home or your job.

Or it could be that there was something you desperately wanted – a child, a qualification, a place on the team, or a promotion – but didn't get? It may be that you're experiencing serious financial difficulties. Perhaps someone you really care about – your partner, child, parent – is struggling with a problem (more on this in the next chapter) and it's having a serious effect on you too. (Someone once told me that you're only as happy as your unhappiest child. It's true.)

Any of these things can leave you feeling sad, lonely and disconnected, anxious, and vulnerable. So can caring long term for someone else – a child, your partner, a sibling, or parent – with a physical or mental illness, or coping with your own physical or mental illness.

Perhaps someone else has badly let you down, betrayed your trust, or cheated on you. Maybe you're persistently being discriminated against, being harassed or bullied. Whatever the issue and the circumstances, when you're going through the kind of event that overwhelms you or even devastates you, the last thing you can imagine is being happy. That's no surprise; it's perfectly normal to feel like that. Sadness and disappointment, shock, and grief are intended to slow you down and allow you to reflect and take in what has happened; to realise that nothing and no one can change what has happened and that you need time to adjust to changed circumstances.

Reach Out to Others
This is possibly a difficult thing to do, but it's crucial. *Reach out* to those you can trust: friends or family who will listen and comfort and/or do something practical to help.

You might want to cope on your own, but pretty much everyone on the resilience courses I teach says that the crucial thing that helped their situation take a more positive direction was the support, encouragement, and comfort of other people. So, whatever you've gone through or are going through, do make sure you get the support you need, whether it's talking with a friend, family member, a help line, or a therapist.

Talk to someone you know who's experienced the same difficulties, or Google a local support group and help line. You'll be able to talk to people who understand what you're going through, and have opportunities to share experiences with others that have been or are going through the same thing – a mental or physical illness, being a carer for someone else, a relationship break-up, bereavement, redundancy, financial problems, etc. – and get information and ideas on how to cope, to move on, or to feel better.

You can also read about how other people have coped; there are others who've made it through and then written books about how you can do it too. Take advantage of their knowledge and experience and get some insight; read blogs and books written by people who've been where you are.

Happiness Habit: Indulge in Comfort and Small Pleasures

For me, happiness comes in tiny, nebulous bursts of gloom-piercing sunbeams.

– Rowan Coleman

It's hard to look forward to each day when you know you will be experiencing pain and sadness. So, each day

(Continued)

127

(*Continued*)

decide to have something to look forward to. Here are some ideas:

- No matter how small it is, have something you can do that you enjoy. Whether it's reading, baking, going for a walk, having lunch with a friend, singing – in a choir or on your own – gardening, doing a crossword, playing computer games – do whatever it is that you like to do.
- Watch an uplifting film, or funny pet videos on YouTube. Look at a book or website with beautiful scenery or beautiful art. Whatever brings you moments of pleasure.
- Listen to music. Music can help you access a range of feelings: anger, sadness, and happiness. Music can soothe or uplift you. Music that you find beautiful and uplifting can provide hope and encouragement.
- If you play an instrument then, if it helps, play that instrument. If you have a hobby or passion that you can 'lose yourself' in, it can help you feel engaged and connected.
- Comfort yourself. Think of pleasant things you can do. Get a massage. Eat healthy comfort food. Wear a favourite piece of clothing. Have a warm bath or a hot shower. Hug or cuddle someone who loves you. Holding hands or walking arm in arm with a friend or family member can comfort and reassure you.
- Do something nice for someone else – a friend, family member, neighbour, or colleague – a small

kindness will take your mind off what you're going through.

- Whatever it is that you get comfort and enjoyment out of, make yourself do it. Do something that gives you pleasure and comfort each and every day.

- Doing things that you enjoy can help you manage difficulties, even if you don't initially feel like doing them. Try your very best to go outside every day, even if it's just stepping out of the front door.

- Do a small chore you've been putting off; reply to an email or text, make an appointment you've been meaning to make. Clean the loo, change a lightbulb, fold or hang up clothes you've left lying around, clear out your coat pockets or bag of receipts, train tickets, etc. Doing a small chore can help you feel that whatever else is going on, you've achieved *something*.

There isn't one right way to take care of yourself when you're going through or you've been through a really difficult experience. When times are tough, what works for you might be different to what works for someone else. And what works for you today might be different to what helped a month ago or in a few months' time.

As the Austrian poet Rainer Maria Rilke said: 'Let everything happen to you: beauty and terror. Just keep going. No feeling is final.'

Happiness Habit:
Look for the Positive

When life feels like it's weighing you down more than normal, it can feel like everything is wrong, bad, or hopeless; there's nothing positive. But there *are* positives – you have to look for them.

Even during the worst of times, there is something to be thankful for. In Chapter 4 you will have read about the idea that every evening, you identify and reflect on three positive things that happened in your day. If you can get into the habit of doing this in your normal daily life, you will have established a habit that will serve you well when you are faced with adversity and really difficult periods in your life.

Every day there is something positive and good. Most of the time it's not obvious. You have to look and, often, you have to look hard. But you can help yourself to cope better in difficult times by training yourself to look for the positive in your everyday life.

Remember, it need only be the small things – this morning's coffee, hearing birds sing in your garden, a funny text from a friend, something good on TV – but it could be the bigger things; maybe you have a good job, or a supportive boss, family, partner, neighbour, or friend.

How Hope Leads to Happiness

(It's) as if all the colours have been washed from your life and it feels like you'll never get them back. I know at this point in time it's difficult to believe that things will ever get better, that you're destined for sadness, but I promise that won't be the case. I've been there, had my whole world turn grey but I've also found that spark again.

– Ellen White

When things are really difficult, when your situation is really tough, it can seem like nothing is going to change; that you won't be able to move on. The thing is, you *can* move on but not until you decide that you *want* to move forward and you *are* going to move on.

Positive change starts with hope. Hope is an inherent aspect of happiness; hope encourages you to believe that things will eventually improve and be good and that you'll feel better.

However, hope is rarely something that just appears; hope is not a switch you can simply turn on. Just like happiness is something you can create, hope is also something you can create. It's within your control to become more hopeful; you have the ability to generate your own hope. How? Well, rather than dwell on what you can't control – which makes you feel hopeless – you start thinking about what you *can* control – which helps you feel hopeful. You take small steps to build your hope up every day by working on the things you do have some control over.

In the same way that you can generate happiness, to generate hope you'll need to set some goals for yourself. Having goals to work towards is one of the best ways to have hope.

In an article for the *Telegraph* newspaper's 'Stella' magazine in 2017, journalist Victoria Young wrote that after the trauma and sadness of six miscarriages, 'it began to dawn on me that I just had to stop waiting to feel better'.

She realised that grief can make you self-centred and that she'd become absorbed in her own little world.

Victoria made a list of steps towards action she could take over the next year.

'I found ways to start thinking about other people. I began volunteering for events at my son's school. I booked afternoons off work to take an elderly friend for a pedicure. When the same friend got ill, I committed to regular visits. I helped out at a community fair … I started exercising … I did something physical every day: walking 10 000 steps, classes in the park, running with mums from the school and sometimes freezing dips in the Ladies' Pond on Hampstead Heath. The physical effects were good, but mentally it was my salvation; no matter how sad or bad I felt, my mood was elevated by doing something physical that forced me into the moment, away from thought.

To combat isolation, I joined a book group. I'd always dismissed such activities as not for me but I needed company. Forced out of my comfort zone of solitude I found that regularly getting together with other women, some of whom I didn't know, was cheering. I also enrolled in a fiction-writing class. Getting lost in other people's lives and tragedies was a great distraction from my own.

I bought a sewing machine, joined a sewing a class, and made curtains and cushion covers. Tapping into my creativity made me feel very gently happy.'

Victoria says she had always been curious about mindfulness, so she did an eight-week course. She found that focusing on the moment was 'a colossal relief'. She also did yoga – she found that she benefited from just being in her body, in the moment, for an hour or two each week – and some counselling: 'Over the course of a year, therapy helped me celebrate the many things I have instead of rueing those I don't.'

Victoria says she realised that 'you don't get over this kind of grief; it's more like a work in progress'. Although time hasn't healed her, she recognises that the things she's done to help her try and feel better have helped the sadness fade.

'For the longest time I couldn't imagine feeling anything other than bleak, sad, and despairing. Then one day, out of the blue, I did. As a result, this new year, I feel more full of hope and happiness than I ever thought possible.'

Although Victoria says that things changed 'out of the blue', it's likely that it was *because* she made changes – positive changes – that gave her control, provided distractions, comfort, and small pleasures – that she was able to feel a lot less bleak, sad, and despairing.

You can do the same: take control; start making small changes that will help begin a shift in your life and give you hope and help you move on. Like Victoria, be open to new ideas and ways of doing things. Think of something or some things you can do – small steps you can take that will enable you to move forward to a brighter future. This is your starting point. Take things one step at a time. Set yourself small, realistic, achievable goals to work towards.

Remember what the philosopher A.C. Grayling says: 'Happiness comes as a sideline of other endeavours that, in themselves, bring satisfaction and a sense of achievement.'

Let Go and Move On

We must embrace pain and burn it as fuel for our journey.
– Kenji Miyazawa

It's too easy to remain unhappy if you're still attached to how things 'should' have been or 'should' be. These expectations are disempowering because, as long as you're trapped in them, you can't move on.

Think about what can be done rather than what can't be done. Rather than think 'It should/it shouldn't have been this way ...' try thinking along the lines of 'It might help to ...', or 'I'm going to try ...', or 'I could ...', or 'now I'm going to ....'

In 2013, when workmen botched the job of building her new home and left her £160 000 out of pocket, it seemed that Carol Sullivan's hopes of transforming her bungalow had been dashed. The builders had bungled the foundations and exterior walls for the new house, leaving a shell that was unsafe and so had to be demolished. Carol tried to get her money back through the courts, but the builders disappeared with nothing in their bank account.

Faced with having to demolish her home and unable to pay someone else to finish the job, Carol decided that the way forward was to build the house in Kempshott, Hampshire, herself. She enrolled on a bricklaying course and began constructing a four-bedroom property from scratch. One year later, having also learnt the basics of plumbing and carpentry, Carol moved into the detached property.

Carol told journalists: 'I knew it would be a huge challenge. Normally a bricklaying course teaches you to build a garden wall, an arch and a chimney breast. I said to the tutors that I'd like to learn how to build a house.'

She put her job as a divorce lawyer on hold to get up at 6 a.m. and spend the day laying bricks from Monday to Friday, with her husband helping her at weekends.

'A year to the day since I started, we moved in', she said. 'At that point the house was just a shell. I did everything from the plumbing to the electrics to the carpentry. The only things I couldn't do were the roofing, levelling the concrete and the plaster work.'

As she said, it was a huge challenge, but Carol knew that every house starts with the first brick; and brick by single brick, if she kept at it, she would get there in the end.

In a Nutshell

- The real challenge to being happy comes when you're stuck in a situation and you can see no way out. It could be that your work is meaningless and dull, but you can't quit. So, what can you do? You can look for the positive aspects of your job and you can make your job work for you; you can create your own meaning and purpose.
- Take charge of your own professional and personal development. Look for ways that you can initiate changes and improvements at work.
- Identify an aspect of your job that is particularly onerous, difficult, boring, etc., then set yourself a challenge to make it less difficult or boring.

- Start working towards your next job – is there a skill you'll need that you can develop in your current job? Think about developing a new skill or an aspect of your job that you're already quite good at or enjoy doing.
- Learn new skills – re-train, study – in your job or in your lunchtime, on your commute, in the evenings or at the weekend.
- There *are* things you can do to make the best out of a bad job. How, though, can you find any happiness when you've suffered or are suffering a serious difficulty? No doubt the last thing you can imagine is being happy.
- Know that sadness and disappointment, shock, and grief are intended to slow you down and allow you to reflect and take in what has happened and have time to adjust to changed circumstances.
- *Reach out* to those you can trust. Do make sure you get the support you need, whether it's talking with a friend, family member, a help line, or a therapist.
- Positive change starts with hope. Hope is an inherent aspect of happiness; hope encourages you to believe that things will eventually improve and be good and that you'll feel better.
- Rather than dwell on what you can't control – which makes you feel hopeless – you need to start thinking about what you *can* control – which helps you feel hopeful. You have the ability to generate your own hope.

(*Continued*)

(*Continued*)

- In the same way that you can generate happiness, to generate hope you'll need to set some goals for yourself. Having goals to work towards is one of the best ways to have hope.
- Be open to new ideas and ways of doing things. Think of something or some things you can do – small steps you can take that will enable you to move forward to a brighter future. This is your starting point. Take things one step at a time. Set yourself small, realistic, achievable goals to work towards.

Happiness Habits

- If you're stuck in a job you don't like, make time in your working day for small pleasures.
- It's hard to look forward to each day when you know you will be experiencing pain and sadness. Whatever it is that you get comfort and enjoyment out of, make yourself do it. Do something that gives you pleasure and comfort each and every day.
- Look for the positives. They might not be obvious – you have to look for them – but even during the most difficult times, there is something to be thankful for.

6
How to Help Others Be Happy

There is no exercise better for the heart than reaching down and lifting people up.

– John Holmes

Having learnt how to help yourself be happier, you might well feel inspired to help others be happier. Is someone you love – a good friend, your partner, parent, son, daughter, or another family member – unhappy? Perhaps they're going through a difficult time – they're upset and feeling miserable for some reason. Maybe they're in an unhappy relationship, they hate their job or where they live. Or they've been bereaved, they're ill, have lost their job, or they have financial difficulties. You can be supportive in these circumstances and help them find their own happiness.

Help Someone Who Is Unhappy

One of the challenges of loving other people is the way our happiness links to their happiness. It's not surprising that when someone you care about is unhappy, you feel it too. In Chapter 4 you'll have read that research shows that emotions are contagious; that happy people positively influence the happiness of those around them. It's also the case that unhappy people negatively influence the happiness of the people around them.

Not only is it troubling and upsetting if someone you love is unhappy, but from a self-centred point of view, it's frustrating; their unhappiness is making you unhappy and you don't want to feel this way. And because you don't want to feel this way, you may find yourself trying to make them feel better just so that you can feel better.

That's not unreasonable, but the more you focus on someone else's unhappiness, the more you risk being dependent on them for your own happiness. You need to separate your feelings from theirs; see your unhappiness about them as separate from their unhappiness.

Whether you just want the other person to be happy so you can be happy, or you genuinely think that you do have all the right answers for them, you cannot make it your mission, your goal, or your project to 'fix' them and make them happy. That doesn't mean to say that you leave them to it, but rather than take responsibility for someone's happiness, you need to support them to find their own happiness; their own solutions. But how do you draw the line between being supportive and taking over, being dragged under, or avoiding the unhappy person? It's not easy to know what to do for the best. Here are some guidelines:

- *Give them the time and space to be unhappy.* People become unhappy for a good reason; as a result of a disappointment, a setback, or something more serious. After a while most people's level of happiness returns to its baseline. Be patient. You often don't need to do anything other than accept how they're feeling and let them know you're there to listen and help if they need you to.
- *Have empathy.* Draw on your own understanding of an experience or situation and on your feelings to help relate to what someone else might be feeling, but keep in mind that they might feel or think differently than you do in any given situation.
- The bottom line with empathy is getting that you might not get it. You don't need to have experienced the same situation as they have, you don't have to agree that you'd feel the same way in the same situation, you just need to recognise the other person's feelings and emotions and realise that, to a greater or lesser extent, they're having a hard time.
- *Don't, though, think you can make someone talk to you.* And don't think they need you around all the time to handle their unhappy feelings. When

people are unhappy, being around them isn't easy, so in giving them space, you give yourself space as well.

- *Learn to recognise the signs.* If the person you care about has regular or frequent dips, learn to recognise the signs. Talk with them when they're in a good place to work out, together, how you can best support them when they're down. The ideas you both have may work, or they may not. If they don't, try other things until you hit on what works best.
- *Suggest professional help.* It might be that the person you care about has, for example, a mental health problem. The mental health charity Mind recognises the challenges of supporting someone you love who is mentally ill. Their information and support page www.mind.org.uk/information-support explains how to cope when supporting someone else and gives practical suggestions for what you can do and where to go for help and support.
- Time to Change – a social movement changing how we all think and act about mental health – also has information to help support a friend or family member. Go to www.time-to-change.org.uk/blog/how-help-friend-who-struggling-their-mental-health.
- *Know your limits.* Don't, though, think that you can make someone get help. Mind says that it's

important to accept that there are always limits to what you can do to support someone else. But they say that accepting what's possible and being aware of your limits can help you feel less helpless.

- *Be your normal, happy self.* It's not just okay to be happy while someone you love is unhappy; it's imperative. The more stable and positive you are, the more likely you're in a position to support and encourage the other person.

Help Someone Be Happy

It may be that the person you care about is looking for ways to move on from unhappiness but doesn't know how. If that's the case there *are* things you can do to help them on the road to happiness. Here are some guidelines.

Help Them to Identify Goals

It's the same for all of us; we all need purpose and meaning in our lives. We need something to work towards; we need goals.

Talk with the other person about what's important to them, what they'd like to work towards. Maybe they want to change their job or career, re-train, or learn new skills. Perhaps they want to leave an unhappy situation – a job or course they hate – or an unhappy relationship.

Whatever goals they might have, get them to think about their answers to the following questions:

- Where are things now in relation to where they want to be; to their goal? What can they already do, what do they already know, and what resources do they currently have in relation to what they need?
- What further information, resources, or help will they need?
- What might the options and opportunities be? What could be the best path to take to work towards achieving their goal or goals?
- What steps could they take towards their goal?
- What would be the first step?

Encourage the other person to commit to specific actions so they can move forward. Help them identify what they can do and to take it one step at a time.

Be Encouraging

Whatever they're aiming for, once they've defined something to aim for – a goal – you can then best help the other person by encouraging them. It could be that they need encouragement to stop doing something – to let go of something – but it could also be that they need encouragement to make a start on something; or to be encouraged to continue to do something despite the difficulties.

Think of a time when you've been encouraged by someone else. Maybe someone simply showed an interest in what you were doing; what you were aiming for or were interested in. Did their encouragement make a positive difference? Do the same for someone else.

Encouragement from you could motivate someone to take a brave step, persist with and complete a difficult task or project, say 'no' to an unnecessary obligation, or do something else that they didn't feel strong enough to do before.

If they're flagging, find out what, exactly, their concerns are. Encouraging someone doesn't mean you deny the difficulties. Instead, acknowledge the challenges and then tell them they *can* manage the difficulties and succeed. Point out what qualities, strengths, and resources they have that will help them to achieve what they're aiming for. Remind them of their reason to achieve something; what they'll gain, how they'll improve themselves or their situation. Get the other person to visualise what success will look and feel like; encourage them to feel and see what's possible; to have a clear picture of what they're aiming for.

Don't, though, wait until they've succeeded or achieved their goal to say something positive. When you see someone making progress, say something; give a compliment or praise. Acknowledge their efforts and point out what they're achieving. If an encouraging thought comes to mind, share it! Don't hold back. Tell them face to face, by text or email.

Give Compliments and Praise

In fact, giving a compliment to someone else can provide a quick boost of happiness; it can make their day, it may even be something they remember for the rest of their life!

There are many reasons you might compliment someone else – it could be they've achieved or overcome something, made a special effort, or put extra time into something that has benefited someone else. It could just be that they're wearing something nice that suits them well. So tell them! You don't need to worry about getting the wording just right. A genuine sentiment phrased a bit awkwardly is better than saying nothing at all.

Start with the reason why you're complimenting or praising the other person. Be specific. Sometimes the most memorable compliments are the most specific ones, because they show that you noticed. For example:

- The way you handled that question at the meeting was perfect. You totally refocused the discussion.
- You've done so well keeping your children entertained during this four-hour delay to our flight!
- You handled that rude customer so well. Well done for being so patient with him.
- What a fab hat! And you wear it so well.
- I love your home! The rug in the living room is beautiful – where's it from?

Look for ways to compliment people for their actions. Acknowledge personal qualities or special efforts: a person's concern and patience or the extra time they put into something. Notice what someone is wearing and how they look. Compliments (appropriate compliments) on appearance make people feel good.

Notice the work someone does. It could be someone who serves you in a shop or café, it could be something about someone's business or someone in your office. Make a positive comment about their work or business.

Take a look around and see who you can pay a compliment to today. If you like something someone has done, has made, is wearing, and so on, don't keep it to yourself. Tell them! Let the other person know that their intentions, efforts, or actions have been noticed and help them feel happy about themselves and their abilities.

Express Your Appreciation

Make an effort to give a sincere thank you to people. Explain the positive difference their efforts have made. People feel good – they feel happy – if they know that they made a difference. So, if what someone has done has had a positive effect on you, explain how. For example:

- Thanks for going out of your way for me; you saved me a lot of time.
- Thanks for suggesting that restaurant. We all enjoyed it so much; we had the best time.
- Thank you for explaining that. You really helped me understand the situation more clearly.

Happiness

Whether it's a friend who's listened to you or a company or individual that's provided a good service, when you tell the other person that they've made a positive difference, they can then feel good about themselves because of the impact their actions had on you.

Show Your Appreciation

When you appreciate and acknowledge someone or something, you recognise the value of something a person has done or given you: their contribution, their time, advice, support. But appreciation can, and often should, be more than simply acknowledging and saying thanks. Saying thanks and expressing appreciation are simply words. But when you *show* appreciation for something, you demonstrate your feelings through actions. You reciprocate; you give in return. It needn't be a grand gesture, just something appropriate that demonstrates your appreciation.

If, for example, a friend mends something for you and it's saved you time, effort, and money, you could bake them a cake or give them a bottle of their favourite drink. And if a family member lends you their car, you could show your appreciation by getting it valeted for them. Again, say thanks and say how it helped make a difference: 'Thanks for fixing my bike/lending me your car – I wouldn't have been able to meet my friends for lunch if you hadn't helped me out. I've baked you a cake/bought you a bottle of wine/got your car cleaned.'

150

Happiness Habit: Be Nice!

Be more aware of other people; their situations and their actions. Look for ways to encourage them, give compliments and praise, express, and show, your appreciation.

Small Pleasures

Since you get more joy out of giving joy to others, you should put a good deal of thought into the happiness that you are able to give.

– Eleanor Roosevelt

Giving encouragement, compliments, and praise, expressing, and showing, appreciation are always things you can do to help make other people happy. There are numerous other small ways you can contribute to others' happiness. You don't have to make big, elaborate gestures; little things that don't take too much effort can make a big difference to someone who could do with a bit of cheer/shot of happiness.

- Start someone else's day with a smile. Send a text tomorrow morning saying 'Morning! How's things with you?'
- Do a chore that you don't normally do for someone else: cook, shop for food, fill or empty the dishwasher, take the rubbish out, clean the loo, get the car cleaned, change the ink cartridge in the printer.

151

- Hide a note for someone you love to find. Just write a simple line of love or encouragement.
- Give a generous tip. Generosity means giving more than might be expected. You have an opportunity to be generous whenever you're aware that extra effort on your part could make all the difference. You can be generous to others with your time, your money, your possessions, with your energy and skills.
- Find an old photo of you and a friend or family member and get it printed and sent to them by an online photo printing company. Try www.photobox. co.uk.
- Send a surprise gift to a friend. When you find something that's easily affordable that you know a friend would like, don't wait for a birthday or Christmas, send it now.
- Write them a card just to let them know you were thinking about them.
- Send a surprise book to someone from an online retailer.
- Is a colleague having a bad day today? Bring them a coffee.
- Offer to help deliver or collect something for someone.
- Be inclusive; encourage others to join you in something; to be involved in what you're doing or talking about.
- Make people feel welcome; let them know that you're pleased to see them: friends and family visiting you at home, clients and customers, new

colleagues at work, new members at a club you belong to.

- Invite people out. Ask someone to do something nice with you: the cinema, a show, a walk, a meal. How often do you make the first move and ask a friend to do something with you? Is it always the other person that organises and invites you out?

- If someone has been telling you about something they hope to achieve and you come across some information relevant to their goal, let them know about it.

- If you hear about an event – an exhibition, a film, a band, pub quiz, a firework display, street party, a new teashop, an 'open garden' – that you think someone you know would enjoy, invite them to it. Ask them if they'd like to go to it with you.

- If someone you know is going through a difficult time, phone or write them a card, email, or text. Cook a meal or send flowers or some other thoughtful expression to let them know you care and are thinking about them.

- At the supermarket, let the person who seems rushed go in front of you.

- Buy someone cake or some fresh fruit – summer strawberries or raspberries. It could be your colleagues, neighbours, family, or friends. Surprise them.

- Provide the best biscuits. If you have someone working in your home – an electrician, plumber, builder, decorator, someone to repair the washing machine – offer them more than a cup of tea. Buy some really nice biscuits and offer those too.

- Give your things away. Have a clear out and give things away to other people via www.freecycle.org.
- Share your knowledge and skills. Has someone expressed an interest in something you're good at – photography, Mexican cooking, website programming, gardening? Share your skills; offer to teach them what you know.
- Leave a positive review. Getting positive reviews can make a big difference to a small business. So, if you had a good time on a vacation or you love your local independent restaurant, leave a positive review. You'll make someone's day.
- Next time you read something that encourages or motivates you, let the writer know. Make a comment on a website or blog; let them know how they helped or inspired you. Write a positive review or comment.
- Whether it's donating money to a friend's www. justgiving.com page for a fundraising event they're involved in or being your friend's gym partner as they try to get fit, helping someone reach a goal will make them happy.
- Let a manager know when you get great customer service. Most of the time, when a customer asks to speak with a manager, it's to complain. This will make two people happy – the employee and the manager.
- Compliment a parent. Let someone you see handling a difficult toddler know that you think they are doing a great job.

- Save a life: donate blood. Donated blood is a lifeline for many people needing long-term treatments, not just in emergencies. Your blood's main components: red cells, plasma, and platelets are vital for many different uses. Go to www.blood.co.uk.
- Help those who need a transplant. Sign up to the organ donor register and donate your organs and tissues. It takes two minutes to fill in the form online. Go to www.organdonation.nhs.uk.

In a Nutshell

- When someone you love and care about is unhappy, you feel it too.
- Whether you just want them to be happy so you can be happy, or you believe that you have the solutions to their problems, you cannot make it your mission to 'fix' them and make them happy. You can, though, be supportive.
- Have empathy. Draw on your own understanding of an experience or situation and on your feelings, but keep in mind that they might feel or think differently than you do. Don't think you can make someone talk to you; give them the time and space to be unhappy.
- Do, though, try and talk with them when they're in a good place to work out together how you can best support them when they're down.
- There are always limits to what you can do to support someone else. Accepting what's possible

(Continued)

(*Continued*)

and being aware of your limits can help you feel less helpless.

- Suggest professional help. But don't think that you can make someone get help.
- Be your normal, happy self. The more stable and positive you are, the more likely you're in a position to support and encourage the other person.
- If the person you care about is looking for ways to move on from unhappiness but doesn't know how, there are things you can do to help them on the road to happiness.
- Help them to identify goals and get them to commit to specific actions so that they can move forward. Help them identify what they can do and encourage them to take it one step at a time.
- Your encouragement could motivate someone to take a brave step and make a start on something or walk away from an unhappy situation. Your encouragement can help them persist with something and complete it, say 'no' to an unnecessary obligation, or do something else that they didn't feel strong enough to do before.
- To encourage someone, acknowledge the challenges but point out what qualities, strengths, and resources they have that will help them to achieve what they're aiming for. Remind them of their reason to achieve something; what they'll gain. Get them to visualise what success will look and feel like. As they make progress, express your admiration and praise.

- Giving a compliment to someone else can provide them with a quick boost of happiness; it can make their day, it may even be something they remember for the rest of their life!
- If you like something someone has done, has made, is wearing, etc., don't keep it to yourself. Tell them. Let the other person know that their intentions, efforts, or actions have been noticed and help them feel happy about themselves and their abilities.
- Express your appreciation. Make an effort to give a sincere thank you to people. Explain the positive difference their efforts have made. People feel good – they feel happy – if they know that they made a difference.
- Don't just express appreciation – show it. It needn't be a grand gesture, just something appropriate that demonstrates your appreciation.
- Contribute to the small pleasures in other people's lives. Little things that don't take too much effort can make a big difference to someone who could do with a bit of cheer or a shot of happiness.

Happiness Habit

- Be aware of opportunities to encourage, compliment, praise, and express and show appreciation for others.

Useful Websites and Books

If you're being bullied or experiencing domestic abuse

www.bullying.co.uk
www.womensaid.org.uk

Ideas for small pleasures

1000AwesomeThings.com

Local interest groups

www.meetup.com

Voluntary work

www.do-it.org

Careers information

nationalcareersservice.direct.gov.uk

Full- and part-time courses

www.hotcourses.com

Information for how to support someone with a mental health issue

www.mind.org.uk/information-support
www.time-to-change.org.uk/blog/how-help-friend-who-struggling-their-mental-health

Books

When to Jump: Mike Lewis
The Top Five Regrets of the Dying: Bronnie Ware
Gone For Lunch. 52 things to do in your lunch break: Laura Archer

Other books by Gill Hasson

Mindfulness: Be mindful. Live in the moment, 9780857084446

Mindfulness Pocketbook: Little exercises for a calmer life, 9780857085894

The Mindfulness Colouring and Activity Book: Calming colouring and de-stressing doodles to focus your busy mind, 9780857086785

Emotional Intelligence: Managing emotions to make a positive impact on your life and career, 9780857085443

Emotional Intelligence Pocketbook: Little exercises for an intuitive life, 9780857087300

Confidence Pocketbook: Little exercises for a self-assured life, 9780857087331

Positive Thinking: Find happiness and achieve your goals through the power of positive thought, 9780857086839

How To Deal With Difficult People: Smart tactics for overcoming the problem people in your life, 9780857085672

Declutter Your Life: How outer order leads to inner calm, 9780857087379

Happiness: How to get into the habit of being happy, 9780857087591

Kindness: Change your life and make the world a kinder place, 9780857087522

Overcoming Anxiety: Reassuring ways to break free from stress and worry and lead a calmer life, 9780857086303

Positive Thinking Pocketbook: Little exercises for a happy and successful life, 9780857087546 (Coming December 2018)

Communication Skills: How to connect with anyone, 9780857087508 (Coming April 2019)

About the Author

Gill Hasson is a teacher, trainer, and writer. She has 20 years' experience in the area of personal development. Her expertise is in the areas of confidence and self-esteem, communication skills, assertiveness, and resilience.

Gill delivers teaching and training for educational organisations, voluntary and business organisations, and the public sector.

Gill is the author of the bestselling *Mindfulness* and *Emotional Intelligence* plus other books on the subjects of dealing with difficult people, resilience, communication skills, and assertiveness.

Gill's particular interest and motivation is in helping people to realise their potential, to live their best life! You can contact Gill via her website www.gillhasson.co.uk or email her at gillhasson@btinternet.com.

Index

achievement, sense of
39, 134
activities, free and
inexpensive 93–5
adolescence 27
alcohol 38
anxiety 4, 38, 69, 126
apologies 17
appreciation
expressing 149–50, 151,
157
showing 150, 151, 157
for things you own 100,
103, 113, 114
for three good things
109–11, 115, 130
Archer, Laura 124–5
Aristotle 12–13, 14, 20, 92
art 42, 93, 112, 128
Auden, W.H. 43

Becker, Joshua 101
being true to yourself 28–9

beliefs, unhelpful 14–20
bird-watching 94
biscuits 153
blood donation 155
boats 100–1
The Body Shop 34
book groups 132–3
books 95, 128, 152
Brault, Robert 17, 111
bullying 75, 126
Burton, Ilona 90, 109, 119
buying things 91–2, 96–7,
98–104, 111–13, 114

cards 152, 153
career changes 50–1
caring for others 126
change 15, 20, 63, 67–8, 83
fear of 64–5, 66
hope leading to 131
'Serenity Prayer' 121
cheap things, buying 102–3
chores 129, 151

Christakis, Nicholas 106
Clooney, George 101
Coleman, Rowan 127
comfort zone, stepping out
    of your 6, 64–7, 81, 83
comforting yourself 128,
    129, 138
commitments, freeing
    yourself from 68–9,
    71–8, 81–3
comparing yourself with
    others 18–19, 21
compliments, giving 147,
    148–9, 151, 154, 157
confidence 8
confirmation bias 120
connecting with others 7,
    56, 105, 107, 113
contagion 106–7, 142
control, taking 75, 131,
    134, 137
cooking 94
courage 78–80, 83, 84
creative interests 42, 95
cultural activities 96
cultural values 27
customer service 154

dancing 95
Davies, W.H. 87
debt 49–50, 71
decluttering your home
    52

depression 4, 38, 40, 69
Diener, Ed 40
difficult times 7, 8, 125–36,
    137–8, 141
    see also setbacks;
    unhappy situations
disability 99
dogs 102
donating blood 155
donating to charity 154
'drains' 105–6, 115
drawing 42, 93
Dunn, Elizabeth 91–2, 102,
    103–4
dwelling on the past 17–18,
    21

emotions 11, 13–14, 15,
    142, 143
empathy 143, 155
encouragement 146–7, 151,
    152, 156, 157
envy 19, 21
eudaimonic happiness 12,
    20, 92
exercise 37–8, 47, 132
experiences 91–2, 96–8, 99,
    105, 111–12, 113

family
    relationships 33, 40
    showing your
        appreciation to 150

support in difficult times
126–7, 137
fear 78, 78, 84
films 95, 128
finances 36–7, 49–50
see also money
first steps, taking 77–8,
79, 82–3, 84
see also step-by-step
approach
flexibility 53, 56–7
Flow 92–3, 94–5, 111, 114
food, giving 150, 153
forgiveness 16–17, 21
Fowler, James 106
Freud, Sigmund 65
friends 33, 40–1, 104–5
letting go of friendships
69, 75
making new 107–8
shared experiences with
105, 113
showing your
appreciation to 150
support in difficult times
126–7, 137
volunteering 114

games 95
Gandhi, Mahatma 25
generosity 152
gifts, giving 150, 152
Girl Guides 44

Girlguiding poll 5
goals 6, 8, 33, 58
alternative options 54
finance-related 36–7
health 37–40
helping others to be
happy 145–6, 154,
156
hope 132, 138
identifying and working
towards 45–53
modifying your 56–7, 59
personal development 42
sharing with others 56
work-related 36
gratitude, showing 149–50,
157
Grayling, A.C. 39, 58, 134
grief 126, 132–4, 137
guilt 15–16, 21

habit, making happiness a
14, 20
health 37–40, 47–8, 108, 126
hedonic happiness 12, 20
helping others
to be happy 7, 8, 16, 21,
141–57
small kindnesses 128–9,
151–5
volunteering 43–5, 108–9,
114
hiring things 101–2, 115

hobbies 41–2, 95, 128
  buying things 98, 112
  making new friends 108
  spending money on others
    104, 113
Hollingworth, James 78
Holmes, John 141
home 37
  building a 135–6
  decluttering your 52
hope 131–4, 137–8

inspiration 80, 84
interests 41–2, 95
  buying things 98, 112
  making new friends 108
  shared 40
  spending money on others
    104, 113
invites, offering 153

jealousy 19, 21
juggling 94

language, learning a 42, 94
letting go 68–70, 79, 84,
    134–6
Lewis, Mike 28
libraries 102
Lincoln, Abraham 3
loneliness 4, 126
Lovegrove, Gilly 93
lunch breaks 124–5

Machell, Ben 110
magic tricks 94
Markham, Ursula 53
Marx, Karl 56
meaning 5, 12, 14,
    33, 66
  goals 45
  values 25
  volunteering 44, 114
  work 122–4, 136
meditation 39
meetup.com 108
memories 97, 112
mental health 4, 38, 108,
    126, 144
Mind (charity) 4, 144–5
mindfulness 90, 133
mistakes, learning from 15
Miyazawa, Kenji 134
money 35, 36–7
  buying things 91–2, 96–7,
    98–104, 111–13, 114
  getting into debt 49–50
  motivation 55, 48, 79
music 41–2, 128

negative people 105–6, 107,
    115
negative thinking 70, 121
Niebuhr, Reinhold 121

optimism 70
organ donation 155

origami 93
overthinking 79, 84
ownership 101

parents 26, 27, 35, 154
Pasricha, Neil 88–9
personal development 42,
    122, 136
personal values 31–2
perspective, getting things in
    80, 84
Phillips, Marie 38–39
photography 93
Plan B, having a 54
planning 54–7, 58, 96, 114
The Pool 38
positive contribution,
    making a 43–5,
    55, 109
positive people 105–6, 107,
    115
positive reviews 154
positive thinking 8, 70–1,
    79, 83, 138
    looking for the positive 130
    stuck in a job you don't
        like 120–1, 136
praise, giving 147, 148–9,
    151, 156, 157
progress, reviewing 56, 59
purpose 5–6, 12, 14, 33, 92
    goals 45
    values 25

volunteering 44, 114
    work 122–4, 136
puzzles 95

'radiators' 105–6, 115
Ratcliffe, Alex 99
reaching out to others
    126–7, 137
reason 12–13, 20
Rees, Dee 27
regrets 15, 29, 64
relationships 8, 33, 40–1
    letting go of draining 75,
        82
    positive 14, 104–8, 113,
        115
    spending money on others
        103–4, 113
    see also family; friends
reminiscing 17–18
responsibility 65–6, 81
reviews, leaving positive 154
Rilke, Rainer Maria 129
risk taking 6, 65, 66, 81
Roddick, Anita 34
Rohn, Jim 11, 63
Roosevelt, Eleanor 151
routines 64, 67

sacrifices 6, 66, 81
sadness 126, 127, 132,
    133–4, 137
Schmich, Mary 104

secondary values 33, 34, 58
self-blame 15
self-esteem 8
Seligman, Martin 13, 14,
    40, 56, 105
'Serenity Prayer' 121
setbacks 53–7, 59, 70
    see also difficult times
shared interests 40
short-lived pleasures 11–12,
    13, 20
singing 95
skills
    developing your 123–4,
        137
    sharing your 154
sleep 99
small pleasures 6, 14, 20,
    87–115
    experiences 91–2, 96–8,
        99, 105, 111–12, 113
    free and inexpensive
        activities 93–5
    helping others 151–5, 157
    looking forward to 127–9
    overcoming grief 134
    positive relationships
        104–8
    volunteering 108–9, 114
    at work 124–5, 138
small steps 50–3, 77, 83,
    131, 134, 138

smiling 90, 114
social media 4–5, 18, 75
social values 31–2, 43, 55
spirituality 42
sports 95, 96, 112
Stadlen, Matthew 94
step-by-step approach 50–3,
    76–8, 83, 131, 134,
    138
stress 4, 8, 39, 69, 119
Sullivan, Carol 135–6
support from others 58,
    106, 126–7, 137

TED talks 123
thanking people 149–50, 157
Time to Change 144

unhappy situations 6, 71–8,
    81–3, 84, 119–38
    helping others to be
        happy 142–5, 155–6
    letting go 68–70
    stuck in a job you don't
        like 120–5, 136–7, 138
    see also difficult times
unhelpful beliefs 14–20

values 6, 25–9, 57,
    66, 114
    goals related to 45
    helping others 43, 44

identifying your core 29,
30–4, 58
secondary 33, 34, 58
sports and cultural
activities 96
work 33–6
volunteering 43–5, 105,
108–9, 114, 132

Ware, Bronnie 29, 64–5, 67
welcoming, being 152–3
wellbeing 11, 12, 20
White, Ellen 131

work 33, 33–6
career changes 50–1
giving compliments 149
stuck in a job you don't
like 120–5, 136–7, 138
working from home
39, 121
working hours 35,
121–2
writing 94, 133

yoga 133
Young, Victoria 132–4